What leaders are saying

"When my parents divorced, I was bewildered that two such good people thought it impossible to live together any longer. The divorce in my church family has been equally bewildering—and just as unnecessary. Thanks to brothers Russell and Atchley for calling all of us in this fractured family to be, at last, reconciled. This is one family reunion I don't want to miss."
—**Leroy Lawson,** *C.M.F. International*

"This is a groundbreaking book in that two leading ministers, from different sides of the aisle, call for reconciliation of their churches after a century of separation. They show tough love in urging, 'It is time to stand united, declare that we are brothers, forget the past, and move forward.'"
—**Leroy Garrett,** *author of* The Stone-Campbell Movement

"In addition to being faithful ministers of the gospel and good friends, Rick Atchley and Bob Russell are peacemakers in the family of God. With remarkable sensitivity and insight, they have carefully built bridges of understanding to reintroduce estranged family members."
—**Jerry Rushford,** *Pepperdine University, Malibu, CA*

"I believe that this joint effort by two of the highest respected preachers in both groups will help readers in both groups to understand each other, our common beliefs and practices, and pave the way for restored fellowship among us."
—**David L. Eubanks,** *President, Johnson Bible College, Knoxville, TN*

"A century has passed since the division that so deeply marked the Stone-Campbell Restoration Movement. Over these years, whenever we have not listened to one another humbly or spoken to one another kindly, we have failed to reflect the spirit of Christ. In this frank and personal book, Atchley and Russell call us back to our greatest commitments—our common faith, our common baptism, our common mission—in hope that we might have a different and more godly future for the sake of God's kingdom."
    —**Jack Reese,** *College of Biblical Studies, Abilene Christian University*

"Bob Russell and Rick Atchley are the ideal team to write this book. Both have integrity, humility, and rock-solid faith. Both are committed to the principles of the Restoration Movement. Both have deliberately reached out to all of God's children through their years of effective ministry. This practical book can be a positive help for all who want to answer our Lord's prayer for unity in His church."
    —**Sam E. Stone,** *Editor Emeritus, The Christian Standard*

"With widening dialogue among our members, congregations, and parachurch ministries, this book will help all of us. It reminds us that we share not only history but theology. We are brothers and sisters in Christ who will be more effective in honoring him as we affirm our unity within God's family."
    —**Rubel Shelly,** *Woodmont Hills Family of God, Nashville, TN*

"Unity. Jesus prayed about this one thesis. Russell and Atchley have nailed it to our door. Such a plea is too marvelous to miss, too glorious to avoid, and too simple to ignore. Could it be that many of our evangelistic methods are but clanging cymbals because we seem deaf to such a courageous charge?"
    —**Terry Rush,** *Memorial Drive Church of Christ, Tulsa, OK*

"By teaming up to write this irenic book, Rick Atchley and Bob Russell have proven that unity is possible and pleasant. You will appreciate their shared convictions on Christ and Scripture, their common passion for oneness and evangelism, and their mutual sense of humor—healing medicine for what ails us."
    —**Victor Knowles,** *Editor, One Body*

"It helps to put things in perspective and that is exactly what Bob Russell and Rick Atchley do in Together Again. They get to the heart of the matter and challenge those of us with roots in the Restoration Movement to examine our attitudes and actions in light of Christ's prayer for unity. The message is a poignant reminder of all we have in common."

—John Derry, *President, Hope International University, Fullerton, CA*

"I can't think of a greater need in our movement than for unity between the Churches of Christ and the Christian Churches. And I can't think of any two preachers who better exemplify the spirit of reconciliation than Rick Atchley and Bob Russell. You need to read this book. The time has come for togetherness."

—Milton Jones, *Northwest Church of Christ, Seattle, WA*

"It takes courage to suggest that our sacred cows have overgrazed the narrow strip of land that separates us. With sensitivity to long-held beliefs, the authors invite us to a barbeque in the lush oasis of unity without compromise. May their tribe increase!"

—Larry Winger, *CEO, Provision Ministry Group*

"With a force mightier than a hurricane, the Holy Spirit of God is on the march again. In this compelling book, Russell and Atchley lead the charge as living examples of how God is reuniting the Christian Church and the Churches of Christ."

—Dudley Rutherford, *Shepherd of the Hills Christian Church, Porter Ranch, CA*

"Rick Atchley and Bob Russell concisely and gracefully call us to embrace the implications of being one in Christ that the world might be won to Christ. May these words walk off the page and into our churches. The Restoration Movement is just that—a movement, not a monument. Thanks, Rick and Bob, for helping us to move forward into the will of God."

—Chris Seidman, *Farmers Branch Church of Christ, Dallas, TX*

"All of us who love God and value unity owe it to the Lord and to ourselves to let the message of *Together Again* take root in our hearts."

—Dick Alexander, *LifeSpring Christian Church, Cincinnati, OH*

"I was born and raised eighteen miles from Ozark Christian College, but I never even knew that wonderful, Christ-honoring school was there because it wasn't 'one of ours.' I can't help but think how much richer my teenage years would have been if we had shared the kind of unity that Rick Atchley and Bob Russell envision in this book. As I read it, I got excited to think about how different that might be in the future. After a century, it's about time!"

—**Mike Cope,** *Highland Church of Christ, Abilene, TX*

"The exemplary church leadership of both Bob Russell and Rick Atchley has been magnified in their exceptional communicative gifts. Together Again is a prophetic call to unqualified unity in Jesus Christ."

—**Ken Idleman,** *President, Ozark Christian College, Joplin, MO*

"Atchley and Russell have acted with courage, voicing out loud the prayers and hopes of many people. May God bless the effort and bring more love into the fellowship of believers."

—**Charme Robarts,** *Skillman Church of Christ, Dallas, TX*

"Taken in total, this book is one of the most balanced treatments of our relationship to other followers of Christ I have seen. What it says about 'Christians only, but not the only Christians' should be read by everyone in our fellowship. Coupled with the authors' treatment of baptism, their approach is one that all of us should be able to live with."

—**Mark A. Taylor,** *Publisher & Editor, Christian Standard*

"We do well to listen when the pulpit ministers of the largest Church of Christ and Christian Church call us to be one in God's family, not because we agree on every doctrinal detail, but because we agree totally on the Lordship of Jesus."

—**Gene Shelburne,** *author of The Quest for Unity*

"Often the hardest part of a conversation is just getting it started. We are all indebted to Bob Russell and Rick Atchley for their efforts to jump-start the conversation among us and point us once more to unity in the Gospel of Christ and our shared mission to preach the Good News."

—**John York,** *Lipscomb University, Nashville, TN*

"God has used Bob and Rick to courageously hold up a light that shows us the wonderful possibility of a unified future. They clearly understand that God has given us a unique moment in time to heal old wounds and begin working side by side in building the kingdom. This book will be a great catalyst in helping many of us to seize the moment!"
—**Jeff Payne,** *Northeast Church of Christ, Taylors, SC*

"I consider it a terrific privilege to recommend this outstanding book by Rick Atchley and Bob Russell—two dear friends and fellow pastors I greatly respect, who are committed to helping bring about the reconciliation of Churches of Christ and Christian Churches and are leading all of us to fulfill the prayer Jesus prayed in John 17."
—**Barry Cameron,** *Crossroads Christian Church, Grand Prairie, TX*

"Kudos to Rick and Bob for initiating a warm discussion that begins to thaw the deep freeze between us. The sad irony, of course, is that our 'Unity Movement' developed rituals and procedures that have made us notorious for drawing lines in the sand and allowing animosity to breed. May God continue to bless their dialogue and give us the courage to believe that 'Unity is Sound Doctrine.'"
—**David Fleer,** *Rochester College, Rochester Hills, MI*

"Russell and Atchley have landed a jetliner in our driveways, and we need to pay attention to this message: The world around us doesn't care whether or not we use instruments and how we organize for missions. They want to know if serving Jesus makes any difference in our lives, our neighborhoods, and the world. So I'm happy to see them reframe the conversation for Restoration churches, leading us to talk more about Jesus Christ and him crucified and resurrected and less about our internal stylistic preferences in worship and organization."
—**Greg Taylor,** *Editor, NEW Wineskins Magazine (www.wineskins.org)*

"Incisive. Enlightening. Inspiring. This little book is all of that and more. The authors really hit the mark in their call to focus on the One who has given us the same core message and mission. A new day has dawned for those of us seeking to honor Christ as we celebrate our unity 'on purpose.'"
—**Alan Ahlgrim,** *Rocky Mountain Christian Church, Longmont, CO*

"The division between God's children has gone on far too long. I thank God that these men are standing up and saying 'enough.' I add my voice to theirs. They have crafted the statement well, giving each individual the right to study, believe, and live in freedom. At the same time they have made it clear that Christ's intention is that we accept as brother and sister all those whom God accepts as children. By tying this to Scripture and to our historical roots, you have done us a great favor."

—**Patrick Mead,** *Rochester Church of Christ, Rochester, MI*

"Bob Russell and Rick Atchley have done both fellowships a wonderful service in their new book. The call for us to unite around the cross is as needed today as it was 200 years ago on the American frontier."

—**Chris Smith,** *Harpeth Hills Church of Christ, Nashville, TN*

"The authors' humble spirit came through the pages loud and clear and is itself a compelling witness of the plea they so eloquently make. This is a compelling message written from the obvious passion of two of the most respected voices among us."

—**John Hampton,** *First Christian Church, Canton, OH*

"Rick and Bob have provided a clear and convincing call for unity between *a cappella* Churches of Christ and the Christian Church. Finally, after one hundred years we're getting Together Again. Nothing can divide us when we focus on Jesus. The authors' plea for unity extends beyond the American Restoration Movement to the unity of all believers. I recommend you provide this book for all the members of your church."

—**Jeff Garrett,** *Norway Avenue Church of Christ, Huntington, WV*

"Rick and Bob have committed themselves to seeing the kingdom of God expand through their ministries. They have both invested their lives in seeing beyond the way things are and leading to what can be. This book will challenge and encourage you to do the same."

—**Rick Rusaw,** *LifeBridge Christian Church, Longmont, CO*

"Wow! What a read! I found this book difficult to put down. It is hard to believe it has taken a hundred years for someone to lead the way in reuniting our churches. Bob Russell and Rick Atchley tell it like it is and do so in a powerful and moving way. This book is going to have an amazing impact on the future of restoration churches."

—**Jim Hackney,** *Heritage Church of Christ, Fort Worth, TX*

"Bob Russell and Rick Atchley, ministers of the largest congregations in their respective fellowships, provide a role model of mutual respect and understanding as they explore their common faith and Restoration heritage and its contemporary relevance. The book is deeply rooted in Scripture and the history and principles of the Restoration Movement. In a sense, this work has taken a hundred years to become a reality as leaders of the two fellowships, sharing a common parentage, search for ways to become reacquainted. It is a must read for restoration minded Christians who care about Christian unity."

—**Lynn McMillon,** *Dean, College of Biblical Studies, Oklahoma Christian University, Edmond, OK*

"Godly men taught me that we should have no fellowship with the 'digressives' in what they deemed the 'conservative Christian church.' I followed their teaching, at first through conscience, but later only because of fear of censure. Over the years I finally came to understand that the best way to honor my teachers was to do just as they taught me: love truth more than tradition. That's why I appreciate this book that calls us to the Biblical truth of treating each other as brothers once again. Besides, since many of my early teachers have gone on to heaven where instruments abound, I figure their fellowship now includes more than just those singing a cappella."

—**Joe Beam,** *Family Dynamics Institute, Franklin, TN*

"You will enjoy Together Again for the same reason you love Reese's Cups: they are a combination of two things you love. Bob and Rick share from the perspective of both fellowships, and I think you'll be hungry for more as you see how God has been busy melting these two great fellowships into a friendship and direction that will never be separated again. Eat up!"

—**Dave Stone,** *Southeast Christian Church, Loiusville, KY*

"In Together Again Rick Atchley and Bob Russell have done a masterful job in describing the common heritage of the a cappella and instrumental branches of the Restoration Movement. But I'm even more inspired by their description of our common destiny as one family. I join these brothers in making the one hundred year anniversary of our split our movement's year of jubilee. Let's forgive one another and come together to fellowship in the name of the Lord. Let us tell the world that we are brethren."

—Danny Sims, *Altamesa Church of Christ, Fort Worth, TX*

"Bob and Rick join their respected voices to speak to 'both sides of the keyboard.' With pastoral sensitivity they help us more deeply appreciate our shared history. More importantly, they prophetically call us to live out a shared future. Here is a vision for a re-united unity movement—a book and a dream whose time has come."

—Ben Cachiaras, *Mountain Christian Church, Joppa, MD*

"Bob Russell and Rick Atchley, two of the most respected, gracious, and influential voices within the Restoration heritage, combine their considerable talents in this landmark book. Their passion for unity among the Churches of Christ and Christian churches is rooted in their love for God, His church, and the Holy Scriptures. This excellent book will be unifying leaven within the Body of Christ."

—Ronnie Norman, *First Colony Church of Christ, Sugarland, TX*

"A beautiful symmetry exists in Rick Atchley and Bob Russell's call for a 'family reunion' in 2006. The terrible schism formally divided the American Restoration Movement 100 years ago—and came about 100 years after the movement's birth. Casting aside the historic barriers between these two churches in that great divide can't come a moment too soon. A world desperate for Jesus Christ awaits."

—Lindy Adams, *former Editor, The Christian Chronicle*

"Bob Russell and Rick Atchley have given us a masterpiece for the encouragement of Christian unity. This book is filled with fine applications of the Scripture, quotes from great men of the faith, and illustrations that are meaningful to the subject matter. I have never found any writing that gives such an understandable and concise history of the reasons that brought about division in our restoration movement. Add to this the fact that it is interesting and inspirational reading and you have a must-read book for every Christian who is interested in the unity Jesus Christ longs for."

—**Ben Merold,** *Harvester Christian Church, St. Charles, MO*

"Thank you, Rick and Bob, for having hearts that allowed God to use you to write a book that is 99 years overdue! May God grant every reader the spirit and wisdom to see a greater sense of unity that He wants for His children."

—**Steve Flatt,** *former President, Lipscomb University, Nashville, TN*

TOGETHER *Again*

RICK ATCHLEY & BOB RUSSELL
TOGETHER *Again*

Restoring Unity in Christ after a Century of Separation

TOGETHER AGAIN
RESTORING UNITY IN CHRIST AFTER A CENTURY OF SEPARATION
Co-published by Leafwood Publishers & Standard Publishing

ISBN 0-7847-1915-2
Printed in the United States of America

Cover design by Rick Gibson
Interior design by Greg Jackson

For information:
Leafwood Publishers, Abilene, Texas
1-877-816-4455
www.leafwoodpublishers.com

Standard Publishing, Cincinnati, Ohio
1-800-543-1353
www.standardpub.com

06 07 08 09 10 11   /   7 6 5 4 3 2 1

DEDICATION

We dedicate this book to the memory of
Thomas and Alexander Campbell, Barton W. Stone,
and the many courageous Restoration pioneers
who envisioned and sacrificed for
the unity of Christ's Body.

Contents

Foreword

"How good and pleasant it is when brothers live together in unity!"
PSALM 133:1

If I am dreaming, please don't wake me now. I have waited fifty years for this. With their new book *Together Again*, Bob Russell and Rick Atchley are moving our hope of Christian unity to a whole new level of nation-wide visibility and grass-roots ownership.

Churches of Christ and Independent Christian Churches have been divided for far too long over far too little. And reunion efforts are not new: Annual joint lectureships in Canada and annual Restoration Forums in the United States have long attracted circles of fine scholars and editors—but made little impact in local church circles. At the end of these events, we went home our separate ways, year after year.

To be sure, we've seen bits of hope below the radar. For example, in the 1960s my Church of Christ father co-shepherded a congregation with a Christian Church elder. At another church planting, one of the two elders serves on the board of a Church of

Christ college, the other on the board of a Christian Church college. I have preached in joint "revival meetings" in both Canada and the United States for forty-five years. In fact, around the globe a few Church of Christ and Christian Church missionaries have quietly partnered for decades.

But something vastly larger is happening these days. *Together Again*, and the events described in it, beckons us along a fresh, hopeful path to unity—through "partnership in the common mission" rather than "polemics about organizational union."

Across my fifty years in ministry I have never sensed the timing to be better and the approach more compelling. Maybe we do have a shot at being "the generation of reconciliation and peace."

Thank you Bob and Rick.

Lynn Anderson
President, Hope Network Ministries,
San Antonio, Texas

Christian unity fascinates me. Could we actually be part of answering Jesus' prayer for His followers to be one? Could we learn to seek the lost and feed the flock instead of battling with other sheep? Could we work together to point others to Jesus, instead of perpetuating unnecessary divisions that only confuse and disillusion honest seekers for truth?

Christian unity convicts and challenges me. It's sad to see so many uncharitable divisions in the Lord's body—even within the

Restoration Movement, which calls us to Christ-centered, mission-focused, Bible-based togetherness in an atmosphere of love. I believe deeply in these principles. Yet, what blessings have I missed because I've neglected my brothers and sisters in the *a cappella* churches of Christ? Have I been part of the problem instead of the solution? Probably so. Have I made "every effort to keep the unity of the Spirit through the bond of peace" (Ephesians 4:3)? Probably not. I want to do better.

Christian unity motivates me. It energizes my prayers, shapes my vision, and fuels my passion for ministry. I want to stand on the Word of God, shoulder to shoulder with all my brothers and sisters. I want to sing and preach the saving grace of Jesus Christ, in harmony with the rest of the body. I want my children and grandchildren to embrace the gospel and communicate it with passion and relevance to the next generation, undistracted by worn-out quarrels.

I'm glad Rick Atchley and Bob Russell got together to write this book. What will happen when millions more of God's people decide to love more deeply, communicate more clearly, and serve the Lord side by side? It's going to be good and pleasant, that's for sure.

David Faust, *President*
Cincinnati Christian University
President, 2006 North American Christian
Convention

A Call for Unity

In the summer of 2003, Bob Russell, minister of the Southeast Christian Church in Louisville, Kentucky, was the president of the North American Christian Convention. It had been a pressure-packed summer for him leading up to the convention with extra meetings to attend, articles to write and speeches to make. Although the convention went great, Bob was relieved to see it come to an end on Friday, July 11. He had circled that day on his calendar as the day the pressure ended and his vacation began. The closing session was Friday morning, and that afternoon Bob was scheduled to play golf in Indianapolis with three other preachers. One of the three was Rick Atchley, minister of the Richland Hills Church of Christ. Rick had attended the convention and had been invited by Bob to teach a class as a special guest from the *a cappella* side of our movement.

Bob, Rick, and the other two preachers headed out to play golf. But on the second hole Bob got an emergency phone call from Mike Breaux, who was at the time the minister of the Southland

Christian Church in Lexington. Mike said, "Bob, I've got an emergency situation at Southland, and I'm not going to be able to preach at Southeast this weekend as I had planned. I'm terribly sorry."

It was Friday afternoon, it was supposed to be the beginning of Bob's vacation, and suddenly the guest speaker for the Sunday services had canceled! Bob wasn't due home until 10:00 p.m. that Friday. He was emotionally exhausted. How could he get a meaningful message together in just a few hours? He started blaming every bad shot he hit for the next couple of holes on Mike Breaux!

Then Bob got a great idea. He turned to Rick and said, "Are you preaching this Sunday or are you on vacation?"

Rick said, "I'm not preaching Sunday, but I'm supposed to fly home tomorrow morning and join my family for a few days with my wife's parents."

Bob said, "Rick, is there any way you could cancel those plans and come preach for us? I know our people would love to hear you!"

"I'd love the opportunity to preach at Southeast," Rick replied. "Let me see what I can do." He made several phone calls, and for the next several holes Rick also blamed Mike Breaux for every bad shot he hit! But finally he said, "I can do it!" and Bob was elated and relieved.

As they continued to play, they talked about the sad irony that two preachers who were well known in their own particular fellowships were such strangers to the other's fellowship—sad because both fellowships shared the same stream of history, a rich heritage sometimes called the American Restoration Movement. The more they talked, the more the Lord birthed in them a desire to see the division between the two fellowships come to an end. They agreed it was time for a "family reunion."

Rick said to Bob, "The best I can determine by reading our history, the division between the two groups was officially recognized in 1906. That means we've bickered and fought as a family for almost a hundred years. Imagine what we could do the next hundred years for our Lord if we reconciled!"

A MOVEMENT OF GOD

In order to understand the split between these two fellowships, you have to know a little bit of history. When Thomas Campbell came to America in the early 1800s, he was an ordained minister in the Old Light Anti-Burgher Seceder Presbyterian Church. On the frontiers of America there were very few Old Light Anti-Burgher Seceder Presbyterians, which fueled a fire that had been burning in his heart since before he left Europe: He was convinced that the denominations of Christianity were petty and counterproductive.

After much searching of Scripture and soul, Thomas Campbell began to speak publicly about his convictions that all Christians should return to a simple form of New Testament Christianity and stand united. In 1809 his dissident teachings got him censured by his Presbytery and finally by the Synod in Western Pennsylvania, but he began to meet with a small group of Christians who also wanted to see the church united. By the fall of 1809, Thomas Campbell had written his *Declaration and Address*, which served as a founding document for what later came to be called the Restoration Movement.

At the same time several other groups on the frontier of America were throwing off their denominational ties and deciding to be just "Christians." One of these groups was led by Barton W. Stone, a Presbyterian minister at Cane Ridge, Kentucky. In 1804 he and several other ministers in the area decided to dissolve their presbytery to unite with all who would become simply Christians and base their beliefs solely on the Word of God. They titled their dissolution letter *The Last Will and Testament of the Springfield Presbytery.*

By the early 1830s the two groups led by Campbell and Stone began to merge and eventually formed what we now call the American Restoration Movement. The movement had a simple plea: Let us unite on Jesus and his Word. "We are not the only Christians," they said, "but Christians only." They rejected creeds and denominational names, believing that such things caused division in the body of Christ. "Where the Bible speaks, we will speak," they said, "and where the Bible is silent, we will be silent." They were convinced that these simple propositions could transform a divided Christianity into a unified church.

For a generation the Restoration Movement made great strides toward unifying all Christians. Not only did thousands of people come to Christ for the first time, but scores of churches also dropped their denominational affiliation, deciding to embrace the restoration ideal and be Christians only. Followers called themselves "Christians" or "Disciples of Christ," and churches changed their names to "Christian Church" or "Church of Christ."

Was the Restoration Movement successful? One historian described the beginning of the Restoration Movement as "the boldest Protestant reformation since the time of Martin Luther," adding that it "spread across the frontier like wildfire, destined to be the most fascinating chapter in America's religious history."[1] And with this rapid growth it maintained for a time a single sense of identity. But that unity began to break down following the Civil War.

A Great Movement Divided

The Civil War not only divided America politically, it also often divided the nation religiously. The war had its impact on this movement as it did on many religious groups, exacerbating theological and methodological differences between the more urban and "progressive" northern churches and the more rural "traditional" southern churches.

An opening wedge of division began with controversy over missionary societies. When the American Christian Missionary Society formed in Cincinnati in 1849, it at first encountered little opposition from church leaders. That changed around the time of the Civil War. Opponents raised several objections: It had become involved in sectional politics during the war, supporting the North; it was an inefficient way to do mission work; it dictated to the churches;

the Bible was silent on church organization beyond the local congregation. Those who supported the society took that silence as
permission. Those who opposed it believed silence prohibited the
formation of a missionary society. Eventually most leaders in the
North supported the Missionary Society and other organizations for
benevolent and mission work. Leaders in the South generally opposed
any organization beyond the local congregation.

    During the same period tension began to emerge over instru-
mental music in worship. The first recorded instance of an
instrument used in worship among the Stone-Campbell churches was
in Midway, Kentucky, in 1859. The minister, L.L. Pinkerton, brought
in a melodeon to help singing that was so bad it "scared even the rats
from worship." In the years that followed it became popular among
the more "progressive" and wealthier congregations to purchase a
piano to use in worship services. But a piano in church reeked of
worldliness to church members in rural southern settings. Previously
only the saloons had pianos. The plunking of a piano reminded too
many of the sounds of the local saloon and made them uncomfortable.

    Those wishing to keep pianos out of the church defended
their position by showing that there were no examples of pianos or
other instruments accompanying worship in the New Testament.
Surely it was proper for them only to sing *a cappella*, and surely those
churches adding pianos were doing so on questionable grounds, they
argued. It was true that the churches with pianos often bought them
because they had become a status symbol of sorts, and regrettably

there was little thought given to the consciences of those who felt uncomfortable with its presence.

The two sides became more and more divided, primarily arguing over the proper understanding of "Where the Bible is silent, we will be silent." One side believed silence meant liberty: There is no law against it, so there is nothing wrong with a piano in the church. The other side contended that silence equaled a prohibition. It was safer, they argued, to focus our attention only on that which is expressly directed in Scripture when we come together to worship God.

Soon the factions were so polarized that they began to fellowship only with those on their side, and to support different missionaries, colleges and publications. The U.S. Census Bureau first officially recognized them as two separate religious groups in 1906. Thus, that is the date—one hundred years ago this year—when the Restoration Movement was officially divided. During this division, most churches in the North became known as Disciples of Christ or Christian Churches; most in the South took the name Churches of Christ.

In the twentieth century, Disciples of Christ divided again, eventually forming two groups: the Christian Church (Disciples of Christ), a more liberal denomination with a national headquarters, and the Christian Churches and Churches of Christ (both names are used), a more conservative and strictly congregational organization. Thus three large Christian groups in America today claim their roots in the Restoration Movement.

A Call for Unity

The synergism of that weekend in 2003 really began with the speech Rick gave at the North American Christian Convention on Thursday night. The theme of the convention was, "I Can Only Imagine." Here is what Rick said that night:

Good evening. This is my first North American Christian Convention, and it has been one of the spiritual highlights of my life. I am about to explode. I don't want it to end! And I can't wait to bring more people back with me again. All week long as I've experienced the convention, I've had mixed emotions. I've been so glad that I could be here, be with you, be blessed by you. But I have to confess that at times I've also caught myself feeling a great sadness.

My name is Rick Atchley. I preach for the Richland Hills Church of Christ in Fort Worth. Some say we're the largest *a cappella* church in America. Until just a few years ago I didn't even know about the convention. I suspect until tonight most of you didn't know about me. Several years ago I spent some time really searching for the heart of God, asking him to give me a mission in the second half of my life that was so big only he could do it. God put something on my heart. I shared it that next Sunday in all three services of our church. I shared with them that God wants me to devote myself for the rest of my life to seeking reconciliation among the *a cappella* churches of Christ and Christian churches of the world.

Over a hundred years ago we split. I don't know what that was all about. I was told when I was a kid that it was about an organ. Now I can't pretend to speak for all of the *a cappella* churches, but I can speak for a lot of them. I know the pulpits of all of our great, growing, thriving churches. I know what those men preach; I know what they don't preach. I know the faculties of our best and healthiest schools. I know what they teach; I know what they don't teach. I know the hearts of the young men and women who are training right now in our schools for ministry—the kind of churches they want to build, the kind of churches they want to be, and the kind of churches they don't want to be. And I can speak for them. And I can tell you tonight, I believe with all my heart that in my lifetime we can have a family reunion.

Now I'm not calling on anyone tonight in any church to change their practices or their preferences. I'm just calling on all of us to recapture the vision of our forefathers of a church that was united simply around the cross of Jesus Christ and ask all the leaders to gather there.

It's going to take several things for this family reunion to take place. We're going to need to do some repenting and some forgiving. Now speaking from the *a cappella* side, it seems to me that we need to do most of the repenting and ask for most of the forgiving. But I'm sure that some of you would say tonight that from your side there have been some things that would have grieved the heart of God too. All I can tell you tonight is that if you've ever heard a sermon, if you've ever seen an attitude by anyone from one of our churches that was ugly, sectarian or cruel, I want to tell you how sorry I am. That's not who we want to be any more. And I'm going to beg you, let's not let old wounds define who we are. Let's let the prayer of Jesus for one body define who we are.

The second thing it's going to take is for us just to reach out to each other. I had no idea what to do three years ago when God put it on my heart, except just to pick up the phone and call the senior minister of the closest Christian Church to me and say, "Let's have lunch and get to know each other." And it's been thrilling to me all week to have so many of you stop and say, "I've become friends with the minister of the *a cappella* Church of Christ in our town, and we're doing things together now." The church where I preach has partnered with some Christian Churches to send a mission team to Uganda that's doing a fantastic work together. And that's where it's got to start. There's no one who can pass an edict or speak for all the churches. It's just going to be you and me reaching out a hand, starting one-to-one with the love of Christ.

And one more thing: We cannot allow a vocal minority to deter us from seeing this dream come true. I have taken considerable criticism from a loud but small group of people for what I've said. And I guarantee you they will get the tape tonight. I can already give you the web sites they will be on by tomorrow. But I am not going to spend the rest of my life intimidated by people who lost the vision our fathers and grandfathers gave their lives for and that, more importantly, Jesus gave his life for.

I can imagine a day—soon—when our preachers are filling each other's pulpits and speaking at each other's conventions. I can imagine a day soon when our churches are partnering together to send mission teams into the world, to do local outreaches in our cities, to feed the hungry, to help the wounded in every major city in America. I can imagine the vision of our Restoration forefathers being restored and the prayer of Jesus being fulfilled. For 100 years we have served God apart. Only God knows what we can do the next 100 years serving him together. But I know this: I know it will be more than we could ask or imagine. Amen.

There is no doubt that Rick's challenge was well received by the attendees of the convention. But it's one thing to applaud a battle plan. It's another to stand on the front lines and charge forward. Lynn Anderson is right when he says we've been separated far too long over far too little.

After one hundred years of division, it is time for a Family Reunion. It is time to put aside our differences and work as one to accomplish Christ's mission to save a lost world. Jesus prayed that we would be one "so that the world may believe that you have sent me" (John 17:21). This book is an effort to explain why we believe the two groups who trace their history to the Restoration Movement and still believe in its founding principles should be unified. We've documented key areas of agreement between the two groups and given practical ideas for steps toward unity in hopes that members of both sides will begin working together for the cause of Christ.

Neither of these two groups has a governing board. We are all members of independent, autonomous churches. The authors of this book hold no official position other than being ministers in our own churches. Christ alone must be our guide, and to him alone we must give account. We pray that Christ will compel and empower each of us that we might usher in a fresh anointing of God's Spirit and a revival of God's people. We pray there will be a renewed emphasis on the unity of all believers, beginning with us, and that we may be one as the Son and the Father are one.

CHAPTER ONE

A Common Plea

A preacher in our movement once spoke to a ministers' meeting where Bob was in attendance. The preacher dogmatically attempted to prove why all the ministers present were wrong on certain doctrines. When he was finished, there was an awkward silence. Bob finally said, "I get the impression that you believe if everyone would just put aside their preconceived ideas and take the Bible for what it is, we'd all agree with everything you just said." He said, "That's right."

How arrogant of us to believe that we alone have a handle on the right doctrine. We've been like the man who wrote,

Believe as I believe, no more no less,

That I am right—no one else—confess!

Feel as I feel, think as I think,

Eat what I eat, drink what I drink,

Look as I look, do always as I do,

Then and only then will I fellowship with you.

The disciple John once said to Jesus, "We saw a man driving out demons in your name and we told him to stop, because he was not one of us" (Mark 9:38). Who did that guy think he was? He hadn't learned the right formula. He didn't have the right education. He wasn't a part of the right circle of followers.

Jesus could have sarcastically noted the irony of the moment. Earlier that same day the disciples had failed to cast out a demon and had to come to Jesus for help. Jesus could have said, "John, I like the way that guy is doing it better than the way you're not doing it!" How often we criticize those who are doing the work of Christ while our own efforts are fruitless! But Jesus patiently corrected him. "Do not stop him," Jesus said. "No one who does a miracle in my name can in the next moment say anything bad about me, for whoever is not against us is for us. I tell you the truth, anyone who gives you a cup of water in my name because you belong to Christ will certainly not lose his reward" (Mark 9:39-41).

That man—the anonymous miracle worker—wasn't a part of the right fellowship. He may not have done the exorcism exactly as the disciples would have. And it is accurate to say that he didn't know as much truth as the disciples because he hadn't been privy to their private conversations with the Master. But he had concluded that Jesus was sent by God, and that Jesus was in a cosmic struggle against Satan. And he took his stand with Jesus against evil in the world.

We don't know how the man became a follower of Christ, but his success proves that his use of the name of Jesus was an expression of faith and not just the invoking of some formula. Later when the sons of Sceva tried to use Jesus' name as a magical prescription to cast out a demon, the demon-possessed man beat them up (Acts 19:13-16). So this man in Mark 9 was a sincere believer, and the fruit of his work proved it.

The disciples wanted to stop him, not because he was a follower of Christ, but because he was not "one of them." Jesus attempted to change their perspective: "He who is not against us is for us." In essence, Jesus was saying, "You guys need to realize you're not the only ones in my camp." This teaching has long been central to the identity of Christian Churches and Churches of Christ.

BOTH FELLOWSHIPS AFFIRM THAT WE ARE NOT THE ONLY CHRISTIANS

The founders of our movement did not consider themselves to be the only Christians.

Thomas Campbell's famous *Declaration and Address* begins with this salutation: "To all that love our Lord Jesus Christ in sincerity, throughout all the Churches." Campbell then refers to them as "Dearly Beloved Brethren." At the time there were no "Independent Christian Churches" or "*a cappella* Churches of Christ," yet Campbell addressed those in the denominational world as his brothers.

His son Alexander Campbell wrote that if there were no Christians in other groups, then "for many centuries there has been no church of Christ, no Christians in the world; and the promises concerning the everlasting kingdom of the Messiah have failed, and the gates of hell have prevailed against his church!" He concluded, "This cannot be; and therefore, there are Christians among the sects."[2]

We don't intend to belittle the importance of our disagreements. People passionately defend the things they hold most dear.

The world doesn't understand why Christians disagree with one another so strongly at times, but it is because they don't value the things we value. Doctrinal purity should be important to followers of Christ. Jesus prayed that we would be united, but he also prayed, "sanctify them by the truth—your Word is truth." It is the truth of God's Word that should unite us.

But a man does not have to be my twin to be my brother. In our disagreements, we should be as siblings who love each other and not as enemies who are out to destroy one another. Accepting someone as a brother does not endorse everything he says or does. It's time we admit that grace had better cover errors in belief as well as practice, or we are all in trouble.

Let's return to Thomas Campbell's simple designation and call those who "love the Lord Jesus Christ in sincerity" our brothers. We will argue just as passionately for our beliefs, and we will seek to unite the churches on the truths of God's Word. But if a group claims to be in submission to the Lord Jesus and sincerely seeks to follow his Word, then let's call them brothers and sisters. Let's do so in the hope and trust that God's grace is sufficient not only to cover a multitude of sins but a multitude of doctrinal errors as well. In other words, let's extend to them the same grace we know we need!

As with the anonymous miracle worker of Mark 9, we should ask, "Are the works of the devil being overcome? Is it being done in Jesus' name, seeking his glory?" If so, then those deeds, and the doers of them, deserve our affirmation, not our opposition. "We are not the only Christians" has been our plea since the beginning, and claiming so has not demanded that we sacrifice our devotion to truth—only our temptation to pride.

Let's be content to be some of God's people without thinking we are the sum of God's people.

BOTH GROUPS AGREE THAT WE SHOULD BE CHRISTIANS ONLY

Though we agree there are Christians in other groups, our two fellowships still long for the day when believers will put aside their denominational distinctions and be known simply as "Christians."

We are grieved that so many believers in Christ tout their denominational name— "I'm Baptist, I'm Nazarene," rather than being simply "Christian." The Bible warns, "One of you says, 'I follow Paul'; another, 'I follow Apollos'; another, 'I follow Cephas'; still another, 'I follow Christ.' Is Christ divided? Was Paul crucified for you? Were you baptized into the name of Paul?" (1 Corinthians 1:12-13).

Paul points out that some of those causing division were saying, "I follow Christ." They were calling themselves Christians only, but were proudly distinguishing themselves from "those denominators."

We have likewise been guilty of hypocritically looking down our noses at our denominational brothers and sisters while proudly maintaining our distinctiveness. We often feel the need to clarify how we are different from other Christians, admitting in the process that we are not truly "Christians only." "Our church is a member of the 'Independent Christian Churches and Churches of Christ,'" we will

say. Or, "We're part of the *a cappella* churches," or "We're affiliated
with this or that convention." In our worst moments of shameful
arrogance, we have even referred to ourselves as "the true church."

Our human nature and pride drive us to distinguish ourselves
from others and join with those who are "like minded." But the battle
is too great! And the call—the plea—is too clear: We must unite with
all believers for the sake of Christ and his Gospel. That means calling
ourselves Christians only, even if we cannot easily distinguish
ourselves from one another or other groups of Christians. After all,
Jesus' charge was not for his followers to argue about how distinct
they are from one another, but to live distinct from the lost with the
goal of leading them to the distinct message of the cross.

Such an understanding was once the foundation of our
movement, going back to the days of Alexander Campbell and Barton
Stone. When the movements led by those two great leaders merged in
1832, it was not because they saw everything alike on all points of
Christian doctrine and practice. They disagreed about names, with
Campbell's followers preferring "disciples," and Stone's using
"Christians." They differed on the frequency of the Lord's Supper. The
"disciples" practiced weekly communion, while the "Christians"
observed communion less often. They differed on views of the Holy
Spirit, which Stone taught played a much larger role in conversion
than Campbell did. There was even a strong divergence of opinion on
the rite of baptism. While both groups practiced baptism by
immersion, most in the Stone movement did not insist it was essential

for the remission of sins, while the Campbell movement did.

Despite these differences, though, Campbell and Stone held each other in high esteem, always attributing to the other the best of motives for the views they held. They shared sincere fellowship with one another, along with a passion for God's Word and a hatred for division. They did not consider their disagreements unimportant or unworthy of further study and continued dialogue. What they considered more important, however, was the unity of the body of Christ. They recognized that their particular movements did not solely comprise Jesus' camp. They were content to be Christians only, but not the only Christians.

We celebrate the revival of such a spirit among our churches today. In fact, we see many similarities between the days when our movement was birthed and today. More and more we notice followers of Jesus growing weary of labels, weary of division, and eager to focus on the battles that really matter. We rejoice that many of the denominational walls that so strongly divided Christians at the beginning of our movement show signs of crumbling, thanks in part to the strong opposition we face in today's world.

Soldiers in the barracks can afford to bicker and fight over card games. But an army on the front lines must stand united against the common foe. Nothing unifies soldiers like a life-threatening enemy. Christians today face such bitter opposition in the world that they are much more likely to forget their denominational baggage and cling to their fellow believers regardless of background. We celebrate this modern-day "restoration" movement that is bringing Christians together in the name of Christ, and we glory in how God has used all things for his good. We call on all believers in our Lord Jesus to set aside petty differences, remove the names that divide us, and call themselves "Christians" only.

A knight appeared before his king and said, "Sire, I have just returned from pillaging and plundering all of your enemies to the east!" The king said, "But I don't have any enemies to the east." The knight replied, "You do now!"

Too often we have fought unnecessary battles and made enemies out of peaceful neighbors. It is time we return to practicing our plea. Let's agree that we are not the only Christians, but Christians only.

CHAPTER TWO

A Common Savior

A teenage girl approached Bob after he had preached a sermon explaining that Jesus is the only way to heaven. Through tears she admitted her frustration. "I can't accept that my friends who don't believe in Jesus are not going to heaven," she said. "It just sounds so exclusive." Her comments reflect the relativistic view of truth so pervasive among her post-modern peers.

Rick had a similar experience recently when he was invited to address a crowd of about four hundred teens from Churches of Christ in a special youth service. They had been instructed a week earlier to write down questions they would like for him to answer. Their number one question—the one they asked three times more than any other—had nothing to do with instruments in worship, the role of elders, or how Jesus was going to return to earth. The question they asked most was, "Why do we think Jesus is the only way to heaven? Isn't that being judgmental of other religions?" These kids were not repudiating Christianity, but were close to repudiating the exclusive plea of Christianity. Influenced by the pluralism of the age, they were wondering if everyone shouldn't be left alone to find whatever spiritual truth works for them.

The times are long gone when Christians can afford to argue about peripheral matters of the faith. It is time to unite to defend the most basic tenets of the faith, and none is more important than this— that Jesus is the Son of God and the only hope for the world. We plead for our movement to lock arms and be on the front lines of this battle.

Both of our fellowships affirm that Jesus is the only way to salvation

As our culture becomes increasingly pluralistic, there is a temptation for us as church leaders to water down the exclusive nature of the Gospel to avoid being labeled intolerant and judgmental. But despite the criticisms we have faced, both of our fellowships still preach that Jesus is the only way to salvation and that only those who surrender to Jesus Christ will be saved. As the world grows increasingly hostile to that message, it will become more and more important that we stand united and say together, "Salvation is found in no one else, for there is no other name under heaven given to men by which we must be saved" (Acts 4:12).

Peter knew that was an "exclusive" position. So did Paul when he wrote, "There is one God and one mediator between God and men, the man Christ Jesus" (1 Timothy 2:5). And apparently the great apostle of love, John, was not concerned about sounding judgmental when he wrote, "He who has the Son has life; he who does not have the Son of God does not have life" (1 John 5:12).

Jesus said, "I am the way, the truth and the life; no man comes to the Father except through me" (John 14:6). The Bible is clear that it is by believing in Jesus Christ and his resurrection, not by unknowingly connecting with his spirit, that a person is saved. For example, Romans 10:9-15 says that a person must hear and believe the message of salvation through Christ in order to be saved:

> That if you confess with your mouth, "Jesus is Lord," and believe in your heart that God raised him from the dead, you will be saved.... As the Scripture says... "Everyone who calls on the name of the Lord will be saved."
>
> How, then, can they call on the one they have not believed in? And how can they believe in the one of whom they have not heard? And how can they hear without someone preaching to them? And how can they preach unless they are sent? As it is written, "How beautiful are the feet of those who bring good news!"

A photographer once asked Bob if there was a way to get on the roof of the church building to take some pictures. "Yes," Bob said. "You have to go through a locked door onto the fifth floor, then you have to enter a code on a keypad lock to get through another series of doors. Then you have to walk through a closet door, climb two ladders and crawl through a small opening that has a padlock on it." Before the photographer could become too discouraged, Bob said, "Why don't I show you the way? I've got the keys, and I've been up there before. Follow me."

When it comes to life after death, we would be smart to follow the One who said, "I've been there before. Come, follow me. I am the way." That may sound exclusive, but if it is the only way, then love demands that we speak the truth.

Rick's personal cell phone number is (817) 891-1234. Actually that's close to the right number, but there are a few digits wrong. What difference does it make? It makes all the difference in the world if you really want to reach Rick! You could say, "I ought to be able to dial any number to reach him. For Rick to allow only one number is so exclusive!" But the one number for Rick separates his phone from all the others. Everyone knows that when you are dialing a cell phone number, truth matters. If there is a right number, it by definition excludes the ten billion other possibilities.

Truth matters not only when dialing a phone number or following directions, but also in aviation, banking, chemistry, athletics and many other fields where the right answer excludes all other possible answers. And truth matters in religion as well. If the core beliefs of different religions about the nature of God and salvation contradict each other, then only one of them can be right, or they are all wrong. There is no other possibility.

There are drastic, irreconcilable differences between Christianity and the other religions of the world. They cannot all be true. There are not many gods—there is only one God: the God of heaven and earth who created us and sent his Son to die for us. And there are not many roads that lead to God—there is only one road: the atoning death of Jesus Christ.

People criticize that message as being intolerant. But

Christianity is not an intolerant faith. The death and resurrection of Jesus were the greatest acts of tolerance in human history. It is by God's grace that we are saved. The atoning death of Christ means that any sin, no matter how great, can be not just tolerated but forgiven by a loving God if we will trust in his one and only Son.

Christianity also is not intolerant because anyone can believe, regardless of race, gender or social status. No one is excluded. Christianity is the most inclusive and most exclusive of all religions. Anyone can believe, but it is only by faith in Jesus Christ that a person is saved. It is that glorious message of salvation through Christ alone that should be our banner and that which unites us. Jesus said, "If I be lifted up, I will draw all men to me." Let our churches be known, then, for their strong and unwavering message about the crucified Christ, the very Son of God!

Both sides agree that it is Jesus Christ whom we should hold high, not our doctrinal distinctions

For the past two hundred years, Churches of Christ and Christian Churches have taken the Lord's Supper weekly. By taking the bread and wine each week, we are called back to the cross, rooted again in the death and resurrection of Jesus as the grounds of our salvation and the central emphasis of our message. We believe it was the practice of the earliest Christians to share the supper of the Lord together each week. By following their example, we are regularly reminded to find our identity in the crucified Christ, and we recommit to following him by dying to ourselves. We rejoice to see many other Christian traditions reexamining the importance of the Lord's Supper and invite all of them to discover the powerful experience of weekly communion with our Savior.

However, at times in the past we have been guilty of preaching our pet doctrines rather than the cross of Christ. We have sometimes left the impression that we are saved by the way we do church instead of the way Jesus made for us at Calvary. But both fellowships agree that we want to be known more for our faithfulness to Jesus Christ than for our stance on baptism or the Lord's Supper. We will communicate our beliefs about those important doctrines, but secondarily to the Gospel itself. It is the Lord Jesus Christ we should hold high, and it is Jesus who will unite us.

This was the clear message in the early days of our movement. For example, consider the words of Robert Richardson, an editor of the *Millennial Harbinger* and personal physician to Alexander Campbell. In 1852 he published a series of articles presenting the basic principles of what he called "the present reformation." He wrote:

We differ from all the parties here in one important particular, to which I wish to call your special attention. It is this: that while they suppose this Christian faith to be doctrinal, we regard it as personal. In other words, they suppose that doctrines, or religious tenets, to be the subject-matter of this faith; we, on the contrary, conceive it to terminate on a person—the LORD JESUS

CHRIST HIMSELF. While they, accordingly, require an elaborate confession from each convert—a confession mainly of a doctrinal and intellectual character, studiously elaborated into an extended formula—we demand only a simple confession of Christ—a heartfelt acknowledgement that Jesus is the Messiah, the Son of God.

The Christian faith, then, in our view, consists not in any theory or system of doctrine, but in a sincere belief in the person and the mission of our Lord Jesus Christ."[3]

If we will place Jesus in the highest place and preach Jesus first and foremost, then other issues will take the lesser place they deserve and will not be so divisive. This will be especially true of the matters that divided us one hundred years ago. Childers, Foster, and Reese, three professors from Abilene Christian University, make this point in their book, *The Crux of the Matter*. They insist that our history is one of too much fragmentation over opinions that are not directly tied to the cross of Christ. They include the controversy over instrumental music in their list of opinions that have unnecessarily divided us. While these scholars from Churches of Christ both affirm and practice *a cappella* worship, they rightly contend that "it is not at the crux of things. Its practice is not tied to the crucifixion and resurrection of Jesus."[4]

At the end of Southeast's "What We Believe" class, Bob often has people call out at the same time the denominational or religious background in which they were raised. It is a discordant sound when dozens of people shout out at the same time, "Catholic," "Presbyterian," "Christian Church," "Baptist," or even "Muslim," "Buddhist," or "Atheist." Then Bob asks them to shout out the name "Jesus," then just whisper together the name of Jesus. You can imagine the sounds of harmony as people say Christ's name in unity.

"When I am lifted up..."—this is the message we call on both our fellowships to herald. When we gather at the cross of Christ, we will find little reason to be cross with each other. Let us together lift up the glorious name of Jesus and proclaim boldly that salvation is found in no other name.

Chapter Three

A Common Truth

Bob and Rick first met in the spring of 2002. Bob was speaking at a Christian Church in Dallas one weekend and was scheduled to speak to leaders of another Christian Church in the area the day before. Rick had become friends with the minister of that church, and when those initial plans had to be changed, the friend suggested that Rick invite Bob to speak to the leaders at Richland Hills Church of Christ instead. Rick admits to being intimidated. "Bob Russell doesn't know me or our congregation," Rick thought. "He's way too busy to bother with a request like that." But the friend insisted, Rick asked, and to his great surprise, Bob agreed to come. Bob met with the leaders of Richland Hills on a Thursday night and greatly encouraged them with his thoughts on characteristics of healthy churches. Rick says, "We all took note of the humility of a man God has used so mightily."

The next day Bob and Rick played a round of golf together. (Both authors agree that golfing together is a great way to promote reconciliation!) As they played Rick asked Bob question after question about things Bob had learned regarding church growth. What impressed Rick most was Bob's strong aversion to any faddish or gimmicky program designed to draw crowds to a church service. Bob put it simply, "I just believe in preaching the Bible. The Word of God alone is powerful enough to draw people." Rick quickly realized the key to the fruitfulness of Bob's ministry—his absolute conviction in the sufficiency of the Word of God! It reminded Rick of a comment he often makes to guests who visit Richland Hills. On many occasions as people have stopped him to praise one thing or another about the church, Rick is quick to say, "Well, we use a good book!"

This has been one of the great strengths of our movement—our high view of the Bible. Together we share a strong conviction to follow God's Word, a conviction that should bring us together.

BOTH FELLOWSHIPS AFFIRM THAT THE BIBLE IS INSPIRED BY GOD AND OUR ONLY GUIDE FOR FAITH AND PRACTICE

"All Scripture is God-breathed," the Bible says (2 Timothy 3:16). We believe that men were "carried along by the Holy Spirit" (2 Peter 1:21) when they wrote the letters and books that are now contained in the canon of Scripture. We believe that God allowed the writers to use their own personality and experience, but that the Holy Spirit guided every word, and that the original words are historically and theologically accurate.

We acknowledge that there have been some scribal errors in the copying of the original manuscripts. And we acknowledge that translators must make certain judgments in translating the Bible from its original languages to any other language. But scribal errors and translations have historically had no influence on the basic doctrines of Christianity. And these minimal points of debate have had nothing to do with the issues that have divided our two fellowships in the past.

Scholars and preachers in both camps consider today's major translations of the Bible to be sufficient for understanding the original, inspired Word of God. No single translation is exclusively inspired. However, we can be thankful that God has used fallible men to translate his infallible Word as accurately as possible into many different languages, and that such translations have brought millions to salvation in Jesus Christ.

BOTH SIDES AGREE THAT WHERE THE BIBLE SPEAKS, WE MUST SPEAK

Bob was invited to be interviewed on Louisville's affiliate of National Public Radio a couple of years ago. The host opened the show like this: "Some say Southeast Christian Church is homophobic, anti-women, exclusive and too concerned about numbers. We'll talk about those things when we come back." Bob was forced to defend his views on many biblical subjects that are considered controversial in our society today.

Rick was recently taken to task in a scathing written attack because he called the practice of homosexuality a sin in the eyes of God. He and his church were charged with being judgmental and hateful. Rick responded by saying that while Christians must love all people, they must also love the truth. It is never loving to stay silent about things that God says he hates.

Because we believe the Bible to be the Word of God, we agree that we must speak God's truth clearly and boldly, even if it is not a popular message today.

We should boldly proclaim the clear doctrines of Scripture. Doctrines like the special creation of man, the sinful nature of man, the virgin birth, the atoning death of Christ, the resurrection, salvation through Christ alone, the second coming of Christ and others must not be compromised. We know of no one on either side of our two movements who denies these doctrines.

We should speak the whole counsel of God regarding matters of salvation. We should preach that salvation comes by God's grace through faith in Christ. We should explain the New Testament directives clearly to those desiring to follow Christ: They are to believe in Christ and his resurrection, repent of their sins, confess the name of Christ, and be baptized into him.

We should follow apostolic precedence in matters of practice and polity. The New Testament does not command us to imitate every practice of the early church. It is not wrong for a church to have its own building rather than meeting only in synagogues and houses as the early church did. It is not wrong for a church to skip a week in taking up an offering, though we've never known one to do so! But as a river is purest at its source, so the church was purest in its infancy. Therefore, we are wise to imitate the early church practices. Though both sides have continued to follow the apostolic examples of weekly observance of the Lord's Supper, governing with a plurality of elders and allowing local autonomy of churches, we need to remember that a precedent does not equal a command. It is important not to divide over disagreements regarding apostolic precedents.

Both fellowships agree that where the Bible is silent, we should be silent

People assume that our split occurred primarily over musical instruments or the missionary society. It may be more accurate to say that these and similar controversies served as a catalyst to divide two camps who already disagreed over the role of the silence of Scripture. The non-instrumentalists argued against the use of instruments in worship based on apostolic precedent since there is no mention of instruments in the corporate worship services of the early church. They felt that a high respect for the silence of the Scriptures meant they should not give license to a practice that the New Testament did not expressly permit. The instrumental side claimed that the same slogan "where the Bible is silent we are silent" gave them liberty to use instruments since there was no New Testament prohibition against their use.

However, neither side is consistent. The non-instrumentalists do not use the same argument of silence to prohibit the use of church buildings, multiple cups, located preachers, orphans' homes, sound systems, pulpits, hymnals or many other things that were not used in the early church. And while they would claim that these additions are mere "expedients," they have been inconsistent in deciding how expedience is determined. This has been the root cause of many of the divisions in Churches of Christ since 1906.

The instrumentalists also have their inconsistencies, since they would not accept that silence means liberty on all occasions. For example, the word "Trinity" is not mentioned in the New Testament. However, a person who rejects the doctrine of the Trinity would not be allowed to preach in Christian Churches because the Scripture so strongly implies that the Father, Son and Holy Spirit are three-in-one and to reject that doctrine is to tear at the very fabric of Christianity. Silence does not always equal liberty.

This is an important point that both our fellowships need to acknowledge. Neither side is consistent on the question of how to interpret silence. Churches of Christ do not believe or practice that everything Scripture fails to mention is forbidden, and Christian Churches certainly do not believe or practice that everything Scripture fails to mention is allowed. Both fellowships use human judgment to make determinations regarding how to interpret the silence of the Scriptures, and it is our disagreements on those interpretations that have been the source of most of our problems.

Our inconsistency on this question has a long history. Consider, for example, the positions of two of our greatest preachers from the 1800s, Moses Lard and J. W. McGarvey. Both men preached against the introduction of instrumental music because the Bible was silent about its practice in the early churches. However, both men endorsed the formation of the missionary society. Why? Because the Bible was silent about the issue, so they refused to make a judgment condemning its creation. It seems that our real problem has never been speaking where the Bible speaks, but remaining silent where the Bible is silent. Too often our motto has been: "Where the Bible speaks, we will speak; where the Bible is silent, we will have even more to say!"

It would be great if we could divide doctrines into two categories: "Doctrines Where the Bible Speaks" and "Doctrines Where the Bible is Silent." We could then agree to allow freedom of disagreement in all matters where the Bible is silent.

But in reality there is a spectrum of clarity regarding Bible doctrines. On one end of the spectrum, "Where the Bible speaks," are doctrines that are so expressly taught in Scripture that anyone who disagrees cannot be said to believe in the inspiration of God's Word. No one who accepts the Bible as true will reject God's creation of man, the atoning death of Christ on the cross, the bodily resurrection of Christ, salvation through faith in Christ, and so forth. Both sides agree, as we mentioned earlier, that regarding such issues, "Where the Bible speaks, we must speak."

On the other end of the spectrum, "Where the Bible is silent," are those issues that have no biblical judgment at all. The size of a church building, whether or not we should use a sound system, the color of the carpet, whether or not the choir wears robes, and an infinite number of other debatable issues fall into this category.

Sam Stone was once preaching at a church in our movement that had suffered a split. When he asked what had caused the split, they said candidly, "The other group believes in fellowship suppers." No matter how bad their hermeneutics might have been, that church quoted Scriptures to support their belief that fellowship suppers were sinful. However, mature believers will agree that we should never divide over such issues.

But then there are important doctrines all along the middle of that spectrum where Scripture may not be clear, but the Bible is not silent either. There may be inferences of Scripture or vague passages but no clear biblical explanation.

Sometimes the Bible is very nearly clear but not explicit. For example, though the New Testament never says so, we agree that abortion is the taking of an innocent human life and contrary to God's will because of biblical inferences. As another example, the Scripture never commands us to believe in inerrancy; however, if "All Scripture is God-breathed," the logical inference is that the words must be true. The closer a doctrine is to the side of the spectrum marked "Where the Bible speaks," the less willing we should be to tolerate the opposing position in the church.

But the issues closer to the middle of that spectrum are the ones that threaten to divide us. With these doctrines, interpretation of Scripture can differ from one Christian to another. Bible-believing Christians can look at the same Scriptures and come to opposing conclusions. The role of women in the church, the title of the preacher, millennial views, and many other issues fall into this category. They are important issues that we should discuss and debate among brothers, but they should not divide us.

Alexander Campbell recognized early on that one of the greatest threats to our movement would be the tendency of people to elevate their judgments on such matters to a level equal to the authority of God's Word. Writing in the *Millennial Harbinger* in 1837, he warned of the problem of "opinionism." Campbell argued that it was not wrong for believers to have opinions, or even to have strongly differing opinions on questions where human interpretations were involved. What was wrong, he said, was the spirit that insisted on propagating one's opinions and demanding that all bow to it. "Opinions in religion can have no authority," he wrote.[5] It was a good word then, and it still is today.

We urge both our fellowships to draw lines based only on what is clearly revealed in the lines of the Bible—and even there to recognize our own inadequacies. Let us stop drawing lines on what we infer or assume to be between the lines of Scripture.

WE AGREE THAT THE USE OF INSTRUMENTS FALLS INTO THE CATEGORY OF "DISPUTABLE MATTERS"

There are inferences of Scripture that both sides have used to prove their point, but both sides must admit that no passage in the New Testament clearly prohibits or permits the use of instruments in worship.

The Bible is clear, however, as to how we are to address such matters: "Each one should be fully convinced in his own mind. He who regards one day as special, does so to the Lord. He who eats meat, eats to the Lord, for he gives thanks to God; and he who abstains, does so to the Lord and gives thanks to God... You, then, why do you judge your brother? Or why do you look down on your brother? For we will all stand before God's judgment seat" (Romans 14:5-11).

We are not to ignore or belittle such disputable matters. On the contrary, we are to personally wrestle with them to the point that we are "fully convinced in our own minds" what is right and wrong. But for the sake of unity, we are not to pass judgment on the one who disagrees with us. "To his own master he stands or falls."

Both of our fellowships have at times had a sectarian spirit regarding the instrument issue. We agree that we should repent of such attitudes and accept this as a disputable matter that should not divide us.

WE AGREE THAT "WEAKER" BROTHERS SHOULD BE RESPECTED, NOT IGNORED

The same passage in Romans 14 also speaks to the response of the "free" person toward those who have a "weaker" conscience regarding these disputable matters: "Accept him whose faith is weak... Therefore let us stop passing judgment on one another. Instead, make up your mind not to put any stumbling block in your brother's way" (Romans 14:1,13).

Paul uses the eating of meat that has been sacrificed to idols as an example. That debate in the early church—over whether or not a person could eat meat that has been sacrificed to idols—has many close parallels to the debates we have waged in our churches over the use of instruments. We could substitute "instrument" for "food" in Romans 14 and gain some helpful insights. Paul continued,

As one who is in the Lord Jesus, I am fully convinced that no food [or instrument] is unclean in itself. But if anyone regards something as unclean, then for him it is unclean. If your brother is distressed because of what you eat [or play], you are no longer acting in love. Do not by your eating [or playing] destroy your brother for whom Christ died.... Let us therefore make every effort to do what leads to peace and to mutual edification. Do not destroy the work of God for the sake of food [or instruments]. (Romans 14:14-20, bracketed words added by the authors)

Surely Paul would say to us, "Do not destroy the work of God for the sake of instruments." How sad it is that so many in our movement one hundred years ago refused to acknowledge the very real violation of conscience that singing with an instrument caused some Christians. It is true that the Bible gives us freedom regarding "disputable matters," and that we should not judge those who exercise that freedom. But it is also true that we should be respectful of those whose sincere effort to please God and seek his truth have led them to believe it is wrong for them to sing with instruments.

What should we do about it? It's difficult to unscramble eggs. It would be terribly unnerving to the members of the instrumental congregations, and in many ways counterproductive, to call on every instrumental church to abandon the instruments in hopes that their non-instrumental brothers might join them.

But at the very least it would be prudent of the instrumentalists to consider the consciences of their brothers when there are joint meetings, of which we hope there will be many in the future. A rapidly growing number of members of *a cappella* churches have no scriptural problem with instrumental worship. Most simply prefer to worship with the human voice alone. However, there are still many sweet brethren in *a cappella* churches who have a sincere conscience problem with worshipping with instruments. Even though they do not wish to deny their instrumental brethren the freedom in Christ to do so, it is a freedom they cannot in good conscience practice. Consider the tension created in the heart of such brothers and sisters when they attend a unity event and are asked to sing worship songs with an instrument playing in the background. To sing along would violate their consciences. To refuse and sit in silence would make them appear sectarian.

The worship leaders of such gatherings must exercise extreme prudence so as not to violate Paul's directives in Romans 14. In many instances, congregational singing in such joint services should be done without instruments. Perhaps a soloist or choir could sing with instrumental background. Perhaps the worship leader could ask all the members of the non-instrumental churches to sing the first stanza of a hymn *a cappella*, then ask only the members of the instrumental churches to sing the second with instruments. Surely there are other creative ways to consider the sensitive consciences of the *a cappella* brothers and sisters. But when calling all Christians to sing together in such services, the worship leader should be prudent and consider silencing the instruments.

WE AGREE THAT WE SHOULD ALLOW FREEDOM
AND NOT CAST JUDGMENT ON DISPUTABLE MATTERS

Though we are calling on the instrumental churches to be sensitive to the consciences of their non-instrumental brothers, we are also calling on the *a cappella* churches to recognize the freedom that we have in Christ.

God's Word says, "It is for freedom that Christ has set us free. Stand firm, then, and do not let yourselves be burdened again by a yoke of slavery" (Galatians 5:1); "You are not under law, but under grace" (Romans 6:14); and, "Now the Lord is the Spirit, and where the Spirit of the Lord is, there is freedom" (Galatians 2:4). One hundred fifty years ago when this debate was first waged, the piano was something most people heard only in the saloons. No wonder so many felt conscience-stricken trying to praise God with a piano in the background. It felt worldly and carnal to them and may have reminded many of their pre-Christian days.

But our culture is different today. Many of us have pianos in our own homes, and our children learn to play instruments at a young age. In such a culture the arguments against a piano in church sound legalistic. Our conscience may be weak in this area because of our traditions, but let us be challenged to acknowledge the freedom we have in Christ and refuse to pass onto our children a strict conviction regarding the use of instruments in worship.

The Old Testament commanded the use of instruments in corporate worship (Psalm 150). We know that Jesus and his disciples worshipped regularly in the Temple where the use of instruments would have been welcomed. There will be instruments in heaven (1 Thessalonians 4:16, Revelation 8:2). It seems unreasonable to conclude that Jesus would have intended the silence of the New Testament regarding use of instruments to be a prohibition. Surely such a departure from the past and future would have demanded a clearer command.

Yes, we should respect those who sincerely have a sensitive conscience in this area. But Paul also warned, "Do not allow what you consider good to be spoken of as evil" (Romans 14:16). We have been set free. Let us not perpetuate into future generations a yoke of slavery. Just as the first-century issue of "eating meat sacrificed to idols" no longer applies to us because the culture has changed, so we hope the day will arrive when the use of instruments in corporate worship is no longer a debatable issue because we all recognize the freedom we have in Christ.

We feel this is important for the health and unity of our churches today. We also feel it is absolutely critical for the future of our movement. Our children in both fellowships are not going to carry this baggage with them any longer. We notice that our young people in instrumental and *a cappella* churches have no interest in this issue, and no desire to perpetuate it. If we desire to see them remain in our movement, we had better start majoring in majors.

We believe that our movement has a great future if we stand on the clear Word of God and allow freedom on matters of opinion. We call on all our churches to speak the truth in love. The words of

Barton Stone are worthy of our consideration:

> The scriptures will never keep together in union
> and fellowship members not in the spirit of the
> scriptures, which spirit is love, peace, unity, forbearance,
> and cheerful obedience. This is the spirit of the great
> Head of the body. I blush for my fellows, who hold up
> the Bible as the bond of union yet make their opinions of
> it tests of fellowship; who plead for the union of all
> Christians; yet refuse fellowship with such as dissent
> from their notions....Such antisectarian-sectarians are
> doing more mischief to the cause and advancement of
> truth, the unity of Christians, and the salvation of the
> world than all the skeptics in the world. In fact, they
> create skeptics.[6]

Let us accept one another without casting judgment. The
unity of the church is a much more important doctrinal issue.

A man who exemplified the posture and attitude we are
recommending was T.B. Larimore, a respected evangelist around the
turn of the twentieth century. At the height of his ministry, Larimore
preached several times a day, averaging over 700 sermons per year
and baptizing thousands of people. He was respected by both sides of
the movement and was often invited by both *a cappella* and instrumental churches to be their guest evangelist even years after the
official 1906 split. Larimore refused to weigh in on the controversies
of the day, calling them "untaught questions among us." "I propose

never to stand identified with one special wing, branch, or party of the church," he said. "My aim is to preach the gospel...."

He was publicly challenged in an open letter to the *Christian Standard* in 1897 to take a stand one way or the other, and he was criticized by both sides as indecisive for refusing to do so. But Larimore responded,

> Never, publicly or privately, have I expressed opinion or preference relative to any of these "matters" ... over which brethren are wrangling and disputing and dividing the church of Christ—NEVER.... I am for Christ, and I believe I can do more for him, his cause and humanity without meddling with these "matters"; hence I let them alone, and just simply "preach the Word," "the gospel of Christ," "the power of God unto salvation."

Larimore insisted that there were good people on both sides, and that it was wrong to assume that the good was all on one side and the bad on the other. "I am as apt to be wrong as my brother," he said. "Neither of us is infallible... I must love my brethren, and never refuse to fellowship them—ANY OF THEM—simply because we do not always understand all questions exactly alike."[7]

This is the spirit of Christ and the Gospel. This is the attitude toward "disputable matters" that will preserve and enhance the unity of Christ's body.

CHAPTER FOUR

A Common Gospel

Both of the authors of this book grew up in Restoration churches where the teaching about the Gospel was unbalanced at times. Bob says, "I grew up listening to preaching that was so strong on baptism that we almost believed in baptismal regeneration—as long as someone got baptized, they were saved." Rick says, "I grew up thinking I was saved, if anyone could know they were saved, because I was in the right church, more than because I was right with Christ. This may not have been the intended message, but it is what many of my generation perceived."

Just before Jesus' return to heaven, he said to his disciples, "Go into all the world and preach the good news to all creation" (Mark 16:15). As the Lord's disciples, our goal is still to go into all the world and preach the Gospel—the "Good News"—that through Jesus Christ we can find salvation from our sins and the promise of eternal life. But that simple Gospel is often misunderstood. People debate about how a person is saved, what a person desiring to be saved should do, and exactly when salvation occurs. The goal of both of our fellowships is to restore the simple New Testament teachings about salvation in a balanced, truthful way.

Both fellowships affirm that it is
by grace through faith that we are saved

The Bible says, "It is by grace you have been saved through faith" (Ephesians 2:8). It is by God's grace, not by being a part of a particular church or submitting to baptism, that a person is saved. It is possible to go to a church that has the right doctrine and still be lost. The Pharisees often had the right doctrine (Matthew 23:3), but Jesus called them children of hell (Matthew 23:15). And it is possible to be baptized and still be lost. A person who submits to baptism ritualistically but has no faith in Christ cannot think he or she will be saved (Mark 16:16, Ephesians 2:8).

Both our fellowships need to acknowledge that in the past we have often misrepresented the gospel message, focusing more on the "pattern" of the church than the cross of Christ. In fact, we have published "gospel" tracts and preached "gospel" sermons that did not even mention the cross! We have often equated the gospel with how to do church instead of what Christ has done.

However, God has always been faithful to raise up bold preachers in our movement to guide us back to the cross whenever we have strayed. Two of those men in Churches of Christ were K. C. Moser (1893-1976) and G. C. Brewer (1883-1956). Both of these courageous evangelists warned their brotherhood of putting more emphasis on the "plan" than the man. In 1945, Brewer wrote,

> To trust a plan is to expect to save yourself by
> your own works. It is to build according to a blueprint;

and if you meet the specifications your building will be approved by the great Inspector! Otherwise you fail to measure up and are lost! That is all wrong, brethren! We have a Savior who saves us. We throw ourselves upon his mercy, put our case in his hands, and submit humbly and gladly to his will. That is our hope and our only hope.[8]

K. C. Moser was also a sharp critic of the "plan" theory. In his 1952 tract titled "Christ Versus a Plan," he argued that much "gospel" preaching among us was not gospel preaching at all. By preaching a plan instead of a man, he claimed that the cross of Christ was being moved from the first place it deserved, and the conditions for salvation given by God were made arbitrary.[9] Men like Brewer, Moser, and others received their share of criticism in their day—proclaimers of grace will always have their detractors—but our movement owes an incredible debt of gratitude to those who would accept no other gospel but the good news of salvation by grace through faith. We are greatly encouraged to see a day where this gospel is now being preached in almost all of our growing churches.

Both sides agree that the Bible gives us clear directives for expressing our faith

In Luke 17, ten lepers came to Jesus for healing. He said to them, "Go, show yourselves to the priests." The Bible says that as they went, they were cleansed (Luke 17:14). When one of the men returned to thank him, Jesus said, "Your faith has made you well" (Luke 17:19).

It was not the action of going to the priest that healed him, but his faith in Christ. Yet his faith was proven in his expression.

A philosopher once said, "An impression without an expression leads to depression." When someone comes to faith in Christ for the first time, he naturally wants to express it. "What must I do to be saved?" was a common question in the early church. The disciples didn't answer that question by saying, "You can do nothing! Just believe! You're already saved!" Neither was the new believer told to raise his hand, fill out a card, or even walk down an aisle.

The Bible gives us clear guidelines for expressing our newfound faith in Jesus Christ. It is by God's grace through our faith that we are saved, but that faith is demonstrated and salvation received when we follow Christ's commands. Our movement has consistently taught, from the days of the evangelist Walter Scott in the 1830s, that the New Testament gives us the following simple steps for expressing our faith in Christ:

Believe. We must believe that Jesus is the Christ, the Son of God (John 3:16), and that God raised him from the dead (Romans 10:9).

Repent. After hearing the first Gospel sermon, members of the crowd in Jerusalem were convicted and asked what they should do. "Repent and be baptized," Peter told them (Acts 2:38). Repentance has to do with a change of direction. It doesn't mean that you must overcome every sin before coming to Christ, only that you are changing your direction and willing to let the Holy Spirit do his sanctifying work in you. If a person claims to have faith in Christ but is unwilling to repent of his sins, we would question the sincerity of that faith just as one would question the faith of one of the lepers had he refused to go show himself to the priest.

Confess. The Bible says, "If you confess with your mouth, 'Jesus is Lord,' and believe in your heart that God raised him from the dead, you will be saved" (Romans 10:9). A believer should publicly confess that Jesus is Lord. By publicly, we do not mean that the confession must be in front of hundreds or thousands. The conversion of the Ethiopian eunuch may have only been witnessed by Philip and the chariot driver (Acts 8:26-40).

Be baptized. Jesus said, "Therefore go and make disciples of all nations, baptizing them in the name of the Father and of the Son and of the Holy Spirit" (Matthew 28:19). Peter said, "Repent and be baptized, every one of you, in the name of Jesus Christ so that your sins may be forgiven. And you will receive the gift of the Holy Spirit. The promise is for you and your children and for all who are far off— for all whom the Lord our God will call" (Acts 2:38).

Both groups affirm baptism as immersion into Christ

Baptism is supposed to be something that unifies Christians. We are thankful to see many other believers in Christ returning to an emphasis on baptism. We see baptism as a participation in the most important events of human history—the death and resurrection of Jesus. Because our emphasis on baptism has often been misunderstood, we have explained below the reasons for our convictions, which are still held strongly in both fellowships.

The Bible says, "Make every effort to keep the unity of the Spirit through the bond of peace. There is one body and one Spirit— just as you were called to one hope when you were called—one Lord, one faith, one baptism; one God and Father of all, who is over all and through all and in all (Ephesians 4:3-6, emphasis added). Yet perhaps no other issue has divided us more often from each other and from other groups of Christians. It is with much hope and prayer that we seek to bring together the many factions in both of our fellowships that have bickered over the place of baptism in the Gospel. We pray that our words will be true to Scripture and will bring unity to the body.

The New Testament form of baptism is immersion. Scholars of every background agree that the Greek word baptizo in New Testament times meant "to immerse, to dip, or to plunge." Romans 6:3-4 says, "Or don't you know that all of us who were baptized into Christ Jesus were baptized into his death? We were therefore buried with him through baptism into death in order that, just as Christ was raised from the dead through the glory of the Father, we too may live a new life." The picture of being buried with Christ is lost if a person is sprinkled. The burial is illustrated only in the original form of immersion. Both of our fellowships practice baptism by immersion.

The New Testament purpose of baptism is to unite with Christ. Every time a person's conversion is detailed in the book of Acts, baptism is an immediate part of the process.

In Acts 2, when Peter preached the Good News to the people of Jerusalem, three thousand responded and were baptized that day (Acts 2:41).

When Philip shared the Good News with the Ethiopian Eunuch, the Scripture says, "They came to some water and the eunuch said, 'Look, here is water. Why shouldn't I be baptized?' And he gave orders to stop the chariot. Then both Philip and the eunuch went down into the water and Philip baptized him" (Acts 8:37-38).

After Saul of Tarsus was blinded by Jesus Christ on the road to Damascus, for three days he fasted and waited for someone to come share the Good News. Ananias came and preached to him, saying, "And now what are you waiting for? Get up, be baptized and wash your sins away, calling on his name" (Acts 22:16). Scales fell off Saul's eyes, and he was baptized before he even ate (Acts 9:18)!

Peter preached the Good News to Cornelius and his household, the first Gentile converts. When the Holy Spirit came upon them, Peter said, "Can anyone keep these people from being baptized with water? They have received the Holy Spirit just as we have." Then Peter "ordered that they be baptized in the name of Jesus Christ" (Acts 10:47-48).

When Paul and Silas were set free from a prison by a miraculous earthquake, they stopped the jailer from committing suicide and shared with him the Good News. Before morning, they had baptized his entire family! The Scripture says, "At that hour of the night the jailer took them and washed their wounds; then immediately he and all his family were baptized" (Acts 16:31-36).

Shortly after the first century, baptism was separated from conversion and infant baptism was introduced. Some denominations still baptize infants, acknowledging that a person's actual commitment to Christ comes much later. Others, noting that baptism in the New Testament always followed a person's faith in Christ, have rejected infant baptism in favor of believers' baptism. But they have often allowed the pendulum to swing to the opposite extreme. Many today baptize believers only after the church is assured that the converts have had adequate training and understand exactly what they are doing, and there may be months between a person's confession of faith and his or her baptism.

But in the early church, such a separation did not exist. Suppose you met a person in the first century who had just given his life to Christ. If you were to ask him exactly when he was saved—was it when he believed or when he was baptized—he wouldn't understand the question. With a confused look he would say, "What does it matter? They happened at the same time. The day I confessed my belief in Jesus I was baptized into his name."

The question would be similar to asking a married couple the exact moment they were married. They could tell you the date of their wedding, but suppose you pressed the point. "Was it when you said 'I do,' or when the preacher pronounced you husband and wife, or when you kissed at the end of the ceremony, or when the marriage was consummated that evening?" They would tell you that it doesn't matter, because all those moments were important, and each one nearly simultaneously led to them being "married."

Because it is our goal to restore the practices of the New Testament church, both fellowships baptize new believers into Christ at the point of their conversion as a part of the salvation process. Baptism is the ceremony that marks the beginning of a person's new life with Christ much like a wedding ceremony marks the beginning of a marriage. Therefore, we speak of baptizing someone "into Christ," borrowing language directly from the New Testament (Romans 6:3, Galatians 3:26-27).

Some judge that such language turns baptism into a work or an attempt to earn God's grace. But that would be similar to judging a person's wedding as an attempt to earn the love of his spouse! We are not claiming that baptism is somehow a "good work" that earns the convert the right to go to heaven. It is instead a humble act of submission to Christ and an expression of the person's newfound faith. Baptism without faith cannot save anyone. But saving faith is expressed in baptism.

The New Testament benefit of baptism is "the remission of sins." Peter told the crowd in Acts 2:38, "Repent and be baptized, every one of you, in the name of Jesus Christ for the forgiveness (KJV – 'remission') of your sins. And you will receive the gift of the Holy Spirit."

Again it must be understood that in New Testament times there was no separation between the moment a person believed and was baptized. In Acts 2:38 Peter mentions repentance and baptism as the point at which a person's sins would be forgiven. But later—when speaking to Cornelius—Peter only mentions belief, saying, "All the prophets testify about [Jesus] that everyone who believes in him receives forgiveness (KJV – 'remission') of sins through his name" (Acts 10:43). Peter was not leaving out baptism and repentance. Later that same day, he baptized those who believed (Acts 10:48). But there was an assumption that repentance, confession, and baptism accompanied belief.

Some outside our fellowship have claimed that we believe in "baptismal regeneration" because we baptize "for the remission of sins." But baptism must be accompanied by faith, repentance, and confession. They are inseparable. We do not believe a person can be saved simply if he or she gets baptized. No one can receive forgiveness of sins apart from faith in Christ. But we do teach that baptism is to accompany that faith and is the ceremonial moment when we receive the assurance that our sins are washed away. Ananias told Paul, "Get up, be baptized and wash your sins away, calling on his name" (Acts 22:16).

In this conviction we stand in the mainstream of historic Christian orthodoxy. The Nicene Creed, still repeated in the worship services of churches all around the globe, confesses that there is "one baptism for the remission of sins." Martin Luther's Small Catechism says that baptism "...effects forgiveness of sins..." The Westminster Confession calls baptism a "sign and seal . . . of forgiveness of sins, and of giving up unto God to walk in newness of life."[10]

The confusion over our view of baptism has been exacerbated

because some in our fellowships have turned this doctrine into a creed, a Shibboleth, judging as heretics those who do not baptize "for the remission of sins." Some have even refused to accept a person's baptism if he came from outside our fellowship, because he was not baptized for the remission of sins. However, this was not the position of our movement's founders, or of key leaders throughout our history.

Around the turn of the twentieth century prominent Southern church leader E. G. Sewell wrote, "There can be no higher motive to move any man to be baptized than to do it for the grand purpose of obeying God, as did Jesus.... So it has long been our custom, when people from the denominations come to unite with us..., to ask them pointedly: 'Are you satisfied that when you were baptized you did it to obey God, to submit to his will?' When they answer in the affirmative that ends the matter with me. We have no right to become judges of their hearts."[11]

David Lipscomb was asked what he would do if he could not convince a potential convert that the remission of sins happened at baptism. He replied, "If I failed to convince him just at what point God pardons his sins, but was satisfied that he was sincerely led by a scriptural motive—the desire of fulfilling all righteousness—I would baptize him. I believe that God would bestow the blessings of the state into which he had entered, just as the man who crossed the line from Kentucky to Tennessee would be entitled to the protection of the laws of Tennessee, even though he might be mistaken as to when he crossed the line."[12]

The questions about when a person receives forgiveness of sins are moot if baptism accompanies faith and repentance. It is only when they are separated that the questions arise. Our goal is to restore the union of baptism and faith and restore the intended picture of baptism. Baptism is joining in the death, burial, and resurrection and receiving the washing away of our sins through the blood of Christ.

WE AGREE THAT CHRIST ALONE
WILL JUDGE BETWEEN THE SAVED AND THE LOST

It is not our job to judge someone's salvation. God alone is the judge. Jesus said, "Whoever believes and is baptized will be saved, but whoever does not believe will be condemned" (Mark 16:16). Condemnation is reserved for those who do not believe in the Son of God. (See also John 3:18.) What about the person who believes but is not baptized? Only God knows the heart, and we know that God will judge justly. There is, however, no excuse for the person who stubbornly refuses to be baptized into Christ. You cannot have faith and be in rebellion at the same time.

Baptism often brings assurance by providing a benchmark for a person's salvation. Many people who were not required to submit to baptism have later questioned their salvation, second-guessing the "experience" they had that brought them to faith in Christ. A person who has publicly confessed that Jesus is Lord and submitted to baptism has the benefit of a benchmark moment when he or she expressed faith in Christ and joined the family of God.

We have experienced such blessings from practicing the ordinance of baptism by immersion that we are surprised that any church would not want to restore this New Testament practice. Baptism is a simple but powerful reminder that our sins are washed away. Public baptisms provide a regular drama for the church of the death, burial, and resurrection of Jesus Christ as a person dies to his sins, is buried in the waters of baptism, and is raised to walk a new life with Jesus.

Rick had a very convicting experience several years ago that has shaped his preaching to this day. Through a mutual friend, he was able to have supper one evening with Rick Warren, well-known pastor of the Saddleback Community Church in southern California. It was sometime in October, and Warren was mentioning that in the past week the Saddleback Church had celebrated its thousandth baptism of the year. The person being baptized was a quadriplegic, and had to be lowered into the baptistry by four people. Warren had pictures of the moment taken, and the following weekend he showed them to his entire congregation. Then he challenged the Saddleback community with these words: "Now if that guy can get baptized, what's keeping you from being baptized?" As Warren spoke, Rick thought to himself, I probably have a stronger view of the necessity of baptism than he does. Why is he preaching baptism harder than I am?

As Rick reflected on that conversation, he came to realize that his repulsion against a gospel of baptismal regeneration, against a sectarian and judgmental gospel, against a legalistic, man-centered gospel, had caused him to become unnecessarily hesitant to call people to be baptized. He recommitted to preaching the gospel of salvation by grace through faith and asking his hearers to express that faith by uniting with Christ through baptism. The result—over sixty people were baptized at Richland Hills in the next few weeks!

Bob and Rick can understand why younger preachers, understandably turned off by sectarian and legalistic preaching, would want to distance themselves from doctrines or practices deemed exclusive or judgmental. But we would call on you to join us in defending the New Testament practices of baptism and weekly communion. While these practices can be preached in a way that is sectarian, they do not have to be. We believe they can be taught and practiced in a way that holds high the cross of Christ, exalting his atoning work as the Good News and only hope of salvation. We also believe they can unite believers. Our heritage has been right to have a high view of these gospel-illustrating ordinances, and we call on the generation of preachers who follow us to continue to give the ordinances the emphasis they have in Scripture.

Southeast Christian Church had a recommitment drive in 2005 in an attempt to clean up their membership role and encourage involvement in the ministry of the body of Christ. At the same time they encouraged hundreds of attendees who had never made professions of faith in Christ and been baptized to do so. The three preachers announced that at least one of them would be at the church building around the clock, ready to baptize people any time during the weekend of October 28 and 29, no appointment necessary. They thought a few dozen might come. Imagine their surprise when a total of 379 people came to be baptized that weekend! Many of them were elderly people who had for years battled a fear of water. One of them, an 89-year-old woman, had never had her head under water! But she was buried with Christ that day and raised to walk a new life with him.

This is the power of the gospel—the true gospel! And if the gospel we preach is true, the cross we hold up will bring us together. In fact, we question the validity of any gospel that keeps believers apart. We call on all churches to return to the simple directives of the New Testament. Let us lead all those desiring to believe in Christ to repent of their sins, confess that Christ is Lord, and be baptized into Christ, that there may again be "one Lord, one faith, one baptism, one God and Father of all."

CHAPTER FIVE

A Common Mission

Bob loves to tell this story about his high school basketball days:

>When I was a senior in high school my goal was to be the leading scorer in Crawford County, Pennsylvania. That was a big deal because every week the top ten scorers were listed in the Meadville Tribune, and you don't get any bigger than the Meadville Tribune!

>All year long I was one of the top three scorers in the county, but there was one problem: One of the two players competing with me for the top position—Jim Komara—was on my team! I can remember many games when we were leading by large margins that Jim Komara took a shot and I was secretly rooting for him to miss!

>But then we got into the state tournament where every game could mean the end of the season and the score was always close. I have to admit that in those games, when Jim shot, I hoped he would make every shot. The goal of winning—the team goal—became more important than my personal goals.

The founders of our movement didn't introduce the idea of restoration for the sake of doctrinal purity alone. They wanted to unite all Christians on the Scriptures for the sake of world evangelism. When we focus on overcoming the real Enemy and winning people for Jesus Christ, then we begin to root for one another. Consider Jesus' prayer in John 17. After praying for his twelve disciples, he prayed for us:

> My prayer is not for them alone. I pray also for those who will believe in me through their message, that all of them may be one, Father, just as you are in me and I am in you. May they also be in us so that the world may believe that you have sent me. I have given them the glory that you gave me, that they may be one as we are one: I in them and you in me. May they be brought to complete unity to let the world know that you sent me and have loved them even as you have loved me (John 17:20-23).

Jesus promised that the world would believe in him if we remained unified. That is why we have such a passion to see our fellowships come together again. This is about so much more than an occasional preacher swap or combined Thanksgiving services. The primary reason we are making efforts to unite our two groups is so that Christ's mission can be accomplished.

BOTH GROUPS DESIRE TO WIN PEOPLE TO CHRIST, NOT EXALT OUR PARTICULAR FELLOWSHIP

A few years ago the *New York Times* reported on the ten fastest

growing religious movements in America during the 1990s. The
Mormons were number one and the Independent Christian Churches
were number two, with over eighteen percent growth. The Restoration
Movement has been experiencing phenomenal growth over the past
fifteen years. New church plants, the explosion of a number of
megachurches, and the significant growth of a number of smaller
churches has resulted in effective evangelism for New Testament
Christianity.

Dr. Jim Garlow, author of *How God Saved Civilization*, is a
respected historian who spoke at a seminar at the North American
Christian Convention in June of 2002. He speculated as to why so
many Restoration churches are growing. His observation has a certain
unbiased credibility because he is not from our movement. He said
that it is very unusual for a movement to stagnate as ours did for a
number of years and then explode in growth. He noted that a few
years ago many church leaders shifted their focus from attempting to
persuade denominations of their errors to trying to win the lost.
Instead of arguing about certain doctrines, churches have lifted up
Jesus Christ, and he is drawing men and women to himself.

When Jesus prayed that we would be one "so that the world
may believe," he was also communicating that if we aren't united,
we'll have a much more difficult time convincing the world to believe
our message. When Christians are divided and bickering with each
other, it negates our influence in the world. The world scoffs at the idea
that Jesus brings peace when we can't even get along with one another.

This is, no doubt, the reason why missionaries from our two fellowships have practiced for years the kind of unity we are calling on our churches in America to embrace. Across the globe our evangelists in other countries recognize that unity is a powerful apologetic. In east Africa, for example, missionaries for *a cappella* and instrumental Restoration churches have worked together for over two decades. Philip Shero, missionary from the *a cappella* side, explains why: "On the mission field, one of the first questions we are asked is, 'Why are there so many different churches? Why can't Christians get along?' When the native peoples see us working together, see the unity of the Spirit on display, it makes our message so much more convincing."

A crusty World War II veteran named M. L. Kapmeyer tells of visiting a prison for the criminally insane. In the prison were well over one hundred neurotic convicts. Kapmeyer observed that there were only three prison guards. He asked the warden, "Don't you worry that the prisoners will join forces and overpower the guards?" The warden's answer was classic: "Oh, no. Lunatics never unite."

Lunatics may never unite, but God's people should. We must unite so that we can "have power to demolish strongholds" (2 Corinthians 10:4). We are commanded,

> Make every effort to keep the unity of the Spirit through the bond of peace... so that the body of Christ may be built up until we all reach unity in the faith and in the knowledge of the Son of God and become mature, attaining to the whole measure of the fullness of Christ.

Then we will no longer be infants, tossed back and forth
by the waves, and blown here and there by every wind of
teaching and by the cunning and craftiness of men in
their deceitful scheming. Instead, speaking the truth in
love, we will in all things grow up into him who is the
Head, that is, Christ. From him the whole body, joined
and held together by every supporting ligament, grows
and builds itself up in love, as each part does its work
(Ephesians 4:3,12-16).

BOTH FELLOWSHIPS ARE WILLING TO WORK TOGETHER TO ACCOMPLISH THE GOAL OF EVANGELISM

If we are working toward the same goal, how foolish of us not
to work together. The opportunity to bring more people into the
Kingdom of God and see more souls saved for eternity should compel
us to put aside our differences and work toward this common goal.

We are not suggesting that our two sides develop an official
missions board that will control all missions dollars. We are simply
suggesting that individual churches on both sides look for ways to
voluntarily cooperate for the purpose of evangelism. This is already
being done here at home and on the mission field with great success.
Here are just a few examples:

Missionaries from both fellowships have been working
together in many places around the world. Richland Hills Church of
Christ supports missionaries in Moscow, Uganda and Kenya who have

cooperated with Christian Church missionaries for years. Manuel de Oliveira, a Church of Christ missionary in Mozambique, lives in a compound with missionaries from Christian Churches. They have planted Restoration churches in every province in Mozambique, where there were none just a few years ago.

Jerry and Aleta Kennedy are missionaries in Cape Town, South Africa, supported by Southeast Christian Church. When they arrived in Cape Town fifteen years ago they began worshipping in an *a cappella* Church of Christ because there were no instrumental churches in the area. They were received so warmly by their *a cappella* brothers and sisters that they are still helping to minister and work among the *a cappella* churches in the Cape Town area today.

We rejoice to hear regularly of churches from both fellowships across the nation cooperating in kingdom-building efforts. Kentucky Christian University has intentionally included faculty and staff from both branches of our movement, and professors from both streams have sometimes joined to present papers or teach seminars both at home and abroad.

First Christian Church in Nashville, Tennessee, recently sold their building to a school and began temporarily meeting at the Woodmont Hills Church of Christ while they were looking for new property. Woodmont Hills was returning the favor, since they met in First Christian's building a few years ago while they were building their new building. Cooperation between the two has been so strong that they have combined college ministries, reaching a number of students from Lipscomb where the Woodmont Hills preacher, John York, is a professor.

One area where we are especially encouraged is in the mission of church planting. In the past year, for example, a Christian Church in Colorado gave money to an *a cappella* church in Texas to plant another *a cappella* church in a nearby town. A dying *a cappella* church in California gave the money from the sale of their building to plant a Christian Church to reach the lost of their community. And in Calgary, Canada, four restoration churches from both fellowships have partnered to plant a new church in the southeast section of their city.

We have heard stories of churches that are serving together in food banks and other ministries to the poor, youth missions and camps, and local outreach efforts. We are convinced that God is honored by such efforts. We are also convinced that we can be far more fruitful together than we can be apart.

When Hurricane Katrina hit New Orleans, Rick's congregation immediately sent a team of people to see what could be done. God showed them favor with city and federal officials, and they were able to set up a camp in a section of the city known as Algiers. Soon they were joined in the effort by Bob's church, and to date hundreds of volunteers from both congregations have spent time together in New Orleans rebuilding houses, cleaning yards, and bringing good news to the citizens there. Dozens of other teams have come from Churches of Christ and Christian Churches across the country. And Jesus' promise has come true: As people have seen these good works, they have glorified the God of heaven.

One of the first churches to join the effort in Algiers was Mountain Christian Church in Joppa, Maryland. Ben Cachiaras, who preaches there, wrote to the Christian Standard about the experience. He mentioned that on the way there the bus broke down close to Natchez, Mississippi. The team of thirteen from Maryland needed a place to spend the night. All the hotels were full. To the rescue came the Fourth Street Church of Christ. Though they were already housing seventy storm evacuees, they gave the group from Joppa a warm meal, a place to sleep, and sincere Christian hospitality. The next day, their bus repaired, the crew from Mountain Christian Church journeyed on to New Orleans.

When they arrived in New Orleans, to identify themselves as a group authorized to enter the site where Richland Hills was working, they were required to post a sign in their windshield that read "Church of Christ." Cachiaras writes:

Our church vehicle has a magnetic sign on it: Mountain Christian Church, Joppa, MD. Isn't it a striking image that a load of people rode into the site with both the Church of Christ and Christian Church labels! The question could be asked, "Well, which are you— Christian Church or Church of Christ?" The answer: Yes. One team. One church. One body. One mission. One Lord. One faith. One baptism.

Jesus' prayer is not mission impossible!

When General Eisenhower was asked how he managed to keep the diverse elements together in the battle of Europe, he said, "Sir, it is one team or we lose." We rejoice in the victories won together. But the enemy is fierce and there are many battles yet to be won. Jesus said that when we're one team, the world will believe and we will win the victory. Otherwise, we may very well lose. Soldiers in the barracks may bicker and fight, but on the battlefield we must stand united. Let's pledge to be one team as we charge forward for the glory of Jesus Christ.

CHAPTER SIX

A Common Bond

Rick tells this story about an encounter with his grandmother that revealed a surprising truth about his heritage:

In the spring of 1987 I had an experience that profoundly shaped my perspective on our movement. I had traveled to Waco, Texas, to visit my grandmother, who was in the hospital fighting the cancer that would take her life a few months later. You need to know that my grandmother, Ona Atchley, is the reason I am a follower of Jesus today. For years she was the only Christian on either side of my family. Her stubborn Abrahamic faith eventually led to the conversion of my grandfather, my father, and my mother. I thank God often for her steadfastness.

As I sat by her hospital bed, I took the opportunity to learn more about her spiritual heritage. I wanted to know more about the faith journey of the woman so responsible for my own. And I wanted to know more about her history with our fellowship in Churches of Christ. Imagine my surprise when she told me something I had never known—that she came to faith as a girl in a small Christian Church in central Texas.

"Are you sure about that, Grandma? I thought you and your family had always been associated with the *a cappella* churches—the Churches of Christ."

"We have been most of my life," Grandma said, "but when I was young, we attended a Christian Church."

"Then when did you and your family leave that church and join the *a cappella* stream of the movement?"

"We never did move," Grandma replied.

"I don't understand, Grandma," I said. "You said you once attended a restoration church that used instruments, but that you started attending an *a cappella* church without moving. That doesn't make sense."

"We didn't move," Grandma explained. "The preacher did."

"What?"

"Well, we had a preacher that liked to sing with instruments, so we did. When he left, we got a new preacher, and he preferred to sing without them, so we stopped."

I couldn't believe my ears. This was probably ten years after 1906, and there were still many churches among us that were refusing to treat this question as something to break fellowship over.

And then it hit me—why did I grow up with such a strong preference for *a cappella* worship? Was it because of a strong theological conviction, a well worked-out hermeneutic? No—I grew up where I did believing like I did because about ninety years ago in a small town in central Texas a preacher moved! If he had not moved, I would have been raised in Christian Churches, gone to a Bible college affiliated with my instrumental brethren—and preached the exact same gospel I preach today!

Jesus could have prayed about many things the night before his death, so it is significant that he chose to pray for unity among his followers (John 17:20). One of the great blessings God desires to pour out on his people is the joy we will experience from being united. The Psalmist wrote,

> How good and pleasant it is when brothers live together in unity!
> It is like precious oil poured on the head,
> running down on the beard,
> running down on Aaron's beard,
> down upon the collar of his robes.
> It is as if the dew of Hermon were falling on Mount Zion.
> For there the LORD bestows his blessing, even life
> forevermore. (Psalm 133)

If God bestows his blessing where brothers meet in unity, is it unreasonable to assume that God would withhold his blessing when brothers refuse to do so?

It was the God-given dream of our Restoration forebears to see the body of Christ live in unity. We were once known as a unity movement, and we rejoice to see a great number of folks in both fellowships eager to be known for that again. Let us have no more to do with the ungodly division that unnecessarily fractured a great move of God. Let us bring the family together again!

BOTH FELLOWSHIPS AFFIRM THAT JESUS CHRIST COMMANDS THE CHURCH TO BE UNITED

The command of Christ that his followers live in unity permeates the pages of the New Testament. We have quoted from many of those passages throughout this book. Paul pleaded,

> If you have any encouragement from being united with Christ, if any comfort from his love, if any fellowship with the Spirit, if any tenderness and compassion, then make my joy complete by being like-minded, having the same love, being one in spirit and purpose (Philippians 2:1-2).

The first proposition of Thomas Campbell's *Declaration and Address* declared, "That the church of Christ upon earth is essentially, intentionally, and constitutionally one." In Ephesians 4:3 Paul said we are to "make every effort to keep the unity of the Spirit." Unity is not something we create. It is the gift of God we are to guard. Proverbs 6:19 says that God hates a man who stirs up dissension among the brothers.

We have fought hard to maintain our doctrinal purity, but we have often failed to maintain one of the most fundamental doctrines of the New Testament: the unity of the church. That's right—unity is sound doctrine! However, we have subordinated this clear doctrine to

less significant ones because they distinguish us from other groups.
We have chosen to divide over many issues that do not rest on nearly
as solid a biblical foundation as the doctrine of unity.

It's time we rekindled a passion for the biblical doctrine of
the unity of all believers. A divided church cannot reach a fractured
world. That's why we are commanded to root out divisiveness:

> But avoid foolish controversies and genealogies
> and arguments and quarrels about the law, because these
> are unprofitable and useless. Warn a divisive person
> once, and then warn him a second time. After that, have
> nothing to do with him. You may be sure that such a man
> is warped and sinful; he is self-condemned. (Titus 3:9-11)

We have been proud of our doctrinal purity, and in our pride
we have ignored one of the Bible's clearest commands. David
Lipscomb said, "There is no sin more frequently and consistently
condemned and warned against as totally evil in its results by both
Christ and the Holy Spirit than that of dividing a church of God."[13]

We agree that our unity must be based upon the Word of
God. In John 17 when Jesus prayed for unity, he also said, "Sanctify
them by the truth; your word is truth" (John 17:17). We would be
opposed to uniting with groups that do not hold high the infallibility
of God's Word. But in our case, both groups strongly believe in the
full authority of the Bible. We are seeking to be unified on God's Truth.
Is not unity a more important doctrine than those that divide us? Is it
not that—unity in truth—which the founders of our movement

dreamed of accomplishing? More importantly, is it not what our Savior wants? How grieved Jesus must be by our petty divisions! How he must long to see us get along as a father longs to see his children loving one another! Unity does not demand a surrender of truth, but it does demand a surrender of pride.

BOTH FELLOWSHIPS ARE OPEN TO PRACTICAL WAYS TO PROMOTE UNITY

The authors of this book have no authority to take any official action regarding our two fellowships. We're just two preachers who want to see God's people unified. Besides, if we are truly non-denominational, there's not a lot of official business we can achieve anyway. What we are proposing is a grass-roots effort to promote and practice unity among the brotherhood churches.

Many are already doing this. Not only are missionaries working together as we mentioned in the last chapter, but there are many relationships being developed between congregations and ministers across the lines of our two groups.

Preaching summits at our Bible colleges have invited preachers from the other fellowship to speak. Elders have been attending one another's leadership conferences. We have heard of in-home Bible fellowships that have joined people from the two groups. Local preachers' meetings have often joined the two fellowships together, and there have been pulpit exchanges. As we mentioned earlier, Rick preached at the weekend services at Southeast a couple of summers ago, and Bob has preached at the Richland Hills Church of Christ. We hope that preachers, Bible college faculty, editors, and small group leaders will all consider ways they can promote unity between our two fellowships.

Real unity, though, will require more practical efforts than preacher exchanges. That's why we're excited to hear about congregations from both fellowships that are going on mission trips together, hosting youth activities together, and working on benevolent projects together. We're excited to hear of leaders encouraging their members to attend workshops and conferences hosted by the other fellowship, as well as men's and women's retreats and seminars. Most of all, we're thrilled to learn of greater cooperation in the mission of reaching the lost, both around the world and at home. We believe God is going to put more dreams like these in the hearts of leaders who truly want to see the harvest increase.

In fact, we believe we are going to see more and more congregations from both groups decide to actually merge with each other for the sake of kingdom effectiveness. This has already happened in places like Irvine, California, Seattle, Washington, and Beaumont, Texas. We are not suggesting that all congregations should do this, or that our two fellowships surrender their own unique identities. However, as more family reunions take place in the future, more of our brethren are going to determine that they can do far more together than they can do apart.

Several years ago the winning horse in a carriage-pulling contest at the famous Calgary Stampede pulled a little over 9,000 pounds. The second-place horse pulled slightly less than 9,000 pounds. After the competition, the owners of those two horses put on a demonstration to show what the horses could do in tandem. Together they pulled nearly 27,000 pounds! The two animals together pulled almost three times as much as one of them could pull alone. There's tremendous power when God's people pull together, too.

BOTH SIDES ARE WILLING TO FORGIVE PAST GRIEVANCES AND UNITE FOR THE SAKE OF CHRIST

It is time to stand united, declare that we are brothers, forget the past, and move forward. In the words of Paul, "Forgetting what is behind and straining toward what is ahead, [let us] press on toward the goal to win the prize for which God has called [us] heavenward in Christ Jesus" (Philippians 3:14). Think of the positive testimony to the world when God's people demonstrate oneness in Christ. To experience the unity for which Christ died, there are several things we need to do:

Repent of divisive attitudes. Several times in this book we've quoted from the passage in Ephesians which begins, "Make every effort to keep the unity of the Spirit through the bond of peace" (Ephesians 4:3). But the preceding verse is vital. Ephesians 4:2 reads, "Be completely humble and gentle; be patient, bearing with one another in love." A prerequisite to unity is a gentle and humble spirit.

We have at times been on the right side of doctrinal issues but had the wrong spirit. Our sectarian spirit has done as much damage as false doctrine. We have seen one another as enemies rather than brothers. We have refused to forgive the divisive spirit of the other. We've been jealous, critical and judgmental. When we're listening to sermons or reading books like this, we often sit poised and ready to pounce on anything we judge to be a doctrinal deviation or homiletical error. We've forgotten that Ephesians 4:15 challenges us to "speak the truth in love." It's been said, "Truth without love is dogmatism; love without truth is sentimentality. Speaking the truth in love is Christianity."

One of the criticisms we have heard of our effort is that we are trying to "apologize" for our respective fellowships. Let us be clear: in no way are we asking churches or brethren to apologize for their preferences or practices in worship, or for following Christ in a way consistent with their own understanding and conscience. Bob has never asked Rick to apologize for worshipping without instruments, nor has Rick ever expected Bob to say he was sorry that he preferred to worship with them. However, both have communicated genuine sorrow to the other for the ugly, caustic, and divisive spirit that has often accompanied the discussion. We do feel each fellowship should apologize to the other for any display of an un-Christlike spirit. And we have regrettably seen such a spirit in both of our fellowships.

The good news, though, is that we are seeing more and more brethren on both sides saying they are repulsed by such a spirit, and no longer willing to see it passed on to their children. Many of us realize that we did not create the division in our movement. We inherited it, and we don't want to pass it on. Earlier in this book, you read Rick's statement to the North American Christian Convention in 2003. His apology and his plea for a family reunion were met with overwhelming gratitude by the thousands gathered. Similar sentiments were expressed at the 1997 NACC by a member of the Christian Church. Victor Knowles, editor of *One Body*, read the following statement to thousands of members of Churches of Christ who were gathered that same evening at a conference in Nashville:

Greetings to the brethren assembled at the Jubilee in Nashville. My name is Victor Knowles and tonight I am speaking at the NACC in Kansas City on the subject, "God's Family, Growing Together in Spirit." I believe that you brethren gathered together in Nashville are a part of the family of God. Wherever God has sons and daughters there I have brothers and sisters in Christ.

My religious heritage is that of the Christian Churches/Churches of Christ. Our two fellowships parted company some ninety-one years ago, mainly over the instrumental music question. I am sorry that the division occurred and deeply regret the separation in fellowship in the subsequent years. Although I was not a part of the original problem, I want to be a part of the healing process. Ninety-one years is too long not to make amends.

I believe the Bible teaches us that we are to be kind to one another, accept one another as God for Christ's sake accepted us, forgive each other, love one another and work together in the kingdom of God. Therefore, please accept one brother's apology for the troubles and heartaches of the past. I am making no judgment as to who was right and who was wrong. I only say that a divisive spirit is wrong and a peaceable spirit is right. I cannot speak for anyone other than myself, but I do believe that I speak the sentiments of many, in fact, the vast majority, in our fellowship.

May God bless all of you in Nashville as together, brothers and sisters in God's family, we grow together in spirit!

Cliff Barrows said there are twelve words that will hold any relationship together: I was wrong, I am sorry, please forgive me, I love you. It's time we spoke these words to one another and allowed the healing to begin.

Encourage one another. To repent means to go in the opposite direction. If we've been divisive, let's begin speaking those words that lead instead to peace and mutual edification.

One of Rick's dear ministry peers in Texas is Barry Cameron, who preaches for the Crossroads Christian Church in south Arlington. Barry has been quick to urge his folks who move to the other side of the county to visit Richland Hills, and Rick has told many of his members moving across town to visit Barry's church instead of making the long drive. Both brothers know their members can be more involved by attending a church closer to their homes, and both are publicly and privately supportive of the option. They are not in competition with each other. They are in a joint struggle with Satan, and are working together to see their county come to Jesus Christ!

Sam Stone, longtime editor of the *Christian Standard*, tells this story:

It was in June 1967 that our family was returning to Cincinnati from a vacation trip up in the Wisconsin Dells. We were driving through Illinois in a rainstorm. Suddenly I saw the car coming toward me start to go sideways in the road. I slammed on my brakes, but I couldn't stop. We crashed in almost a head-on collision. One person was killed in the other car. My wife was the most seriously injured in ours. She had a skull fracture and was taken to the intensive care unit at the nearby hospital in Bloomington. My boys both escaped injury and a nurse from the emergency room took them home with her until my brother-in-law could come from Chicago to get them.

In the impact, my head hit the steering wheel and my glasses were shattered. The doctors removed 21 pieces of glass from my eyes. They had put medicine in my eyes and I had them bandaged, so I couldn't see.

Here I was in a strange town, many miles from home, my boys were with someone I didn't know, my wife down the hall fighting for her life in the intensive care unit. The first person to come to visit me took my hand. I'll never forget that handshake. "Brother Stone?" I said, "Yes." And he introduced himself and told me that he was an elder in the church of Christ there. He had heard on television about the accident and the newscast had said that I was minister with the Western Hills Church of Christ in Cincinnati. He wanted to see if he could help.

As we talked, I explained that the church where I served was one of the churches of Christ that did use instrumental music. He said, "I thought that might be— but that doesn't matter. We just want to help a brother in Christ." And help they did. Their elders brought communion to my wife during her two weeks in the hospital; their church sent flowers to us; they kept our relatives in their homes; and I stayed in their home for several days after being released until Gwen was able to travel. And I was reminded that we were all a part of one family—God' family. I pray that every one of us might reach out to each other as that brother did to me, with a handshake of Christian love, as together we seek to keep the unity of the Spirit in the bond of peace.

Be positive about our movement. Some of us have suffered from a poor self-image about our movement. We're always thinking the grass is greener on the other side of the denominational fence. If you

have traveled overseas, you have probably discovered that the more
you see of other countries, the more you appreciate the United States.
In the same way, the more we see of other religious movements, the
more attractive ours becomes.

The minister of a large Christian Church admitted he no
longer affiliates himself with our movement. He sees no need for a
convention or communication among the brotherhood churches since
we aren't a denomination. The usual answers didn't compel him. The
revival spirit that draws many to our conventions doesn't attract his
people because they enjoy great worship and teaching every week. It
wasn't important to him that they know the great history of our
movement. And more importantly, he was concerned that the
members of his church, who were excited about being a part of a free,
non-denominational church, would be turned off by some in our
movement whom he considered legalistic, sectarian and mean spirited.
He knew his people would be discouraged by that spirit and say,
"Why are we a part of that? I thought we were non-denominational!"
So he has phased his congregation out of all affiliation with our
movement.

We understand his concerns. For those same reasons, many
young church planters with roots in Churches of Christ are also
distancing themselves from any affiliation with their heritage. It is
true that some in every camp of our movement have been legalistic,
sectarian and mean spirited. And it's true that such a spirit has done
great harm to the body of Christ and to the goals of our movement.

Our movement's forefathers envisioned a day when the Restoration Movement would no longer be necessary because all Christians would have united on Christ and his Word. Great progress has been made, but the goal has not yet been accomplished. We don't think God is finished yet with the Restoration Movement.

Forty years ago Dr. Lewis Foster predicted, "We're going to come to a time in Christendom when we aren't divided by denomination. We'll be divided between those who believe in the lordship of Christ and the inspiration of the Scriptures, and those who don't." That time has come. Kennon Callahan, a church growth expert, speaking to an interdenominational conference of ministers, began by saying, "The day of denominationalism is dead."

As a non-denominational movement, we're in an ideal position to reach those who are turned off by the politics of organized religions. We don't have to win people to the teachings of Alexander Campbell or Barton Stone. They are attracted to our basic plea. "We stand firm on Scripture, but have freedom in opinion. We have no official creeds—we just want to exalt Christ. We don't claim to be the only Christians, but that's our only name—Christian." What a wonderful plea! Let's be positive about it.

Have a sense of humor. When Rick spoke at Southeast, Bob introduced him as being from the Richland Hills Church of Christ. Bob said, "At Richland Hills they sing without instruments. They have a worship team that is outstanding. In fact, we hope to have them here sometime. But here we sing with instruments—the way God intended!"

People knew he was teasing and they laughed. Rick felt more at ease and teased Bob back. The Bible says, "A merry heart does good like medicine" (Proverbs 17:22a, KJV). Let's keep our sense of humor.

Be sensitive to both sides. Bob says that a few years ago a forum met at Southeast that involved people from non-instrumental churches. They decided to stay and participate in the Wednesday night service. Bob didn't know ahead of time that the representatives were going to be there, and he didn't know exactly what the service was going to be like. The service was one of the most edgy Wednesday night services they had ever had. Bob felt uncomfortable the whole time, wishing they had planned a milder worship service to be sensitive to the guests.

When we participate in services together, let's be sensitive. Not only should we respect the consciences of those who do not sing with instruments, when we meet with each other we are wise not to see how much we can get by with.

Courageously withstand the criticism. It is impossible to avoid every word of criticism. Nehemiah had his Sanballat and Tobiah. Jesus had his Pharisees and Sadducees. The critics we will always have with us. But let's not be held hostage by them. Do not be intimidated by the fault-finders. Ninety-five percent of the people in the pews of our congregations are anxious to put aside petty differences and get on with the task of impacting our world for Jesus Christ. Those of us who lead churches, Bible colleges, publishing houses, periodicals and missions need to have the courage to politely thank the critics for their input, then continue on.

Several years ago ten whales were found beached on the Baja Peninsula. Rescue efforts were too late and they all died. At first marine biologists were puzzled and unable to explain the senseless loss of life. However, their investigation revealed a simple, yet sad scenario. Newspapers reported their conclusions with this headline: "Giants perish while chasing minnows." Apparently, the whales lost their focus and beached themselves while chasing fish they could never catch in such shallow water. The cause of Christ is too great to be "beached" while we major in minors or argue with those who choose to do so. Let us not be distracted by the loud but small minority of brethren who would spend all their time in the shallow water. Let's pray for them, but stay in the deep!

Be patient. Change doesn't happen overnight. The issues that have divided us for a hundred years will not be easily overcome. Think about the issue of circumcision in the New Testament church. Even though Simon Peter had communicated clearly with Cornelius that circumcision was not necessary, years later the issue surfaced again. Paul said he had to confront Peter to his face because of his attitude toward the Gentiles. Attitudes take a long time to change, and we must be willing to exercise great patience and perseverance in our efforts toward unity.

Exalt Jesus Christ, not ourselves. Often the reason we struggle to accept those who disagree with us is that we are hesitant to accept the radical implications of God's grace. It is difficult to set aside our pride and admit it is by grace we are saved, not by moral or theological perfection. "Accept one another, then, just as Christ accepted you, in order to bring praise to God" (Romans 15:7).

We are saved by Christ, not correctness. If that's true, then we can accept someone whose doctrine isn't perfectly aligned with ours. Someone said, "If we spent more time at the cross of Jesus, we would spend less time being cross with each other! Let's accept that a man doesn't have to be my twin to be my brother. Let's admit that none of us has achieved doctrinal perfection, and let's be thankful that we're saved by grace.

If you're in a fierce battle, it doesn't matter much if a fellow soldier is in a different platoon, shoots with his left hand, whistles a contemporary tune or wears an earring. What matters is that he shoots in the right direction. Jesus said, "Whoever is not against me is for me." It's time to mean it when we sing,

We are not divided,

All one body we,

One in hope and doctrine,

One in charity.

A few years ago when the present building of Southeast Christian Church was under construction, a group of staff members went out to the site to watch the fifty-foot cross being set in place at the top of the fifty-foot high building. They stood in the unfinished balcony and peered through the beams of the roof as a huge crane began to lift that cross from the ground higher and higher until it eventually was dangling over a hundred feet in the air. As the crane slowly lifted the cross in place, the staff members noticed that the construction workers with their hard hats had stopped to watch the cross. A group of church members stood on the ground taking pictures. Several cars stopped along the street and drivers stuck their heads out the windows, watching the cross. An elderly couple walking their dog stopped to watch the cross being set in place. A photographer from the local newspaper was there taking pictures of the cross. It was a visual demonstration of Jesus' promise, "If I be lifted up, I will draw all men to me."

We can't manufacture unity. We can't transform people's lives. We can't save the world. But Jesus Christ can. If we will just lift him up, if we will just speak the truth with a humble, loving spirit, he will draw all men to himself and we will be one in him.

Rise up O Church of God!

His kingdom tarries long.

Bring in the day of brotherhood

And end the night of wrong.

Notes

1 Louis and Bess Cochran, *Captives of the Word* (Garden City, NY: Doubleday, 1969).

2 Alexander Campbell, "Any Christians Among Protestant Parties?" *Millennial Harbinger* (September 1837), 411-13.

3 Robert Richardson, *Principles of the Reformation*, edited and introduced by Carson Reed (1850; reprint ed., Siloam Springs, AR: Leafwood Publishers, 2002), 44.

4 Jeff Childers, Douglas Foster, and Jack Reese, *The Crux of the Matter: Crisis, Tradition and the Future of Churches of Christ* (Abilene, TX: ACU Press, 2001), 247.

5 Alexander Campbell, "An Indictment of Opinionism," *Millennial Harbinger* (1837).

6 Barton Stone, "Remarks," *Christian Messenger* 9 (August 1835), 180.

7 C. Leonard Allen, *Distant Voices: Discovering a Forgotten Past for a Changing Church* (Abilene, TX: ACU Press, 1993), 153-159.

8 G. C. Brewer, "Confession and the Plan of Salvation," *Gospel Advocate* 87 (April 26, 1945), 233.

9 K. C. Moser, *Christ Versus a "Plan"* (Searcy, AR: Harding College Bookstore, 1952).

10 *Creeds of the Churches*, edited by John H. Leith, 3rd Edition (Atlanta: John Knox, 1982), 33, 120, 224. For indepth treatment of this mainstream viewpoint, see John Mark Hicks and Greg Taylor, *Down in the River to Pray: Revisioning Baptism as God's Transforming Power* (Siloam Springs, AR: Leafwood Publishers, 2004).

11 E. G. Sewell, *Gospel Advocate* (December 17, 1903), 809.

12 David Lipscomb, *Salvation from Sin* (Nashville, TN: Gospel Advocate, 1913), 233.

13 David Lipscomb, "Queries," *Gospel Advocate* 22 (29 January 1880), 69.

Resources for Further Reading

Foster, Douglas, and Gary Holloway. *Renewing God's People: A Concise History of Churches of Christ.* Abilene, TX: ACU Press, 2001.

Encyclopedia of the Stone-Campbell Movement. Edited by Paul Blowers, Anthony Dunnavant, Douglas Foster, and Newell Williams. Grand Rapids, MI: Eerdmans, 2005.

Garrett, Leroy. *The Stone-Campbell Movement.* Joplin, MO: College Press, 1994.

Knowles, Victor. *Together in Christ: More Than a Dream.* Joplin, MO: College Press; Abilene, TX: Leafwood Publishers, 2006.

Murch, James DeForest. *Christians Only: A History of the Restoration Movement.* Cincinnati, OH: Standard Publishing, 1962.

North, James B. *Union in Truth: An Interpretive History of the Restoration Movement.* Cincinnati, OH: Standard Publishing, 1994.

One Body Magazine. Edited by Victor Knowles.

Webb, Henry E. *In Search of Christian Unity.* 1991; New edition, Abilene, TX: ACU Press, 2001

ACKNOWLEDGEMENTS

The authors wish to thank Rusty Russell for listening, compiling, and shaping our thoughts through the use of his God-given gifts. We also want to thank Gary Holloway of Lipscomb University for his assistance and Leonard Allen, our editor, for his helpful suggestions.

Rick Atchley & Bob Russell